# Prozac

## North American Culture and the Wonder Drug

# ANTIDEPRESSANTS

Antidepressants and Advertising: Marketing Happiness

Antidepressants and Psychology: Talk Therapy vs. Medication

Antidepressants and Social Anxiety: A Pill for Shyness?

Antidepressants and Suicide: When Treatment Kills

Antidepressants and the Critics: Cure-Alls or Unnatural Poisons?

Antidepressants and the Pharmaceutical Companies:
Corporate Responsibilities

Antidepressants and Their Side Effects: Managing the Risks

The Development of Antidepressants: The Chemistry of Depression

The Future of Antidepressants: The New Wave of Research

The History of Depression: The Mind-Body Connection

"Natural" Alternatives to Antidepressants:
St. John's Wort, Kava Kava, and Others

Prozac: North American Culture and the Wonder Drug

Psychostimulants as Antidepressants: Worth the Risk?

*ANTIDEPRESSANTS*

**Prozac**

*North American Culture and the Wonder Drug*

by Joan Esherick

Mason Crest Publishers

Philadelphia

Mason Crest Publishers Inc.
370 Reed Road
Broomall, Pennsylvania 19008
(866) MCP-BOOK (toll free)

Copyright © 2007 by Mason Crest Publishers. All rights reserved. No part of this publication may be reproduced or transmitted in any form or by any means, electronic or mechanical, including photocopying, recording, taping, or any information storage and retrieval system, without permission from the publisher.

First printing
1 2 3 4 5 6 7 8 9 10

Library of Congress Cataloging-in-Publication Data

Esherick, Joan.
  Prozac : North American culture and the wonder drug / by Joan Esherick.
    p. cm. — (Antidepressants)
  Includes bibliographical references and index.
  ISBN 1-4222-0106-6    ISBN (series) 1-4222-0094-9
  1. Fluoxetine—Juvenile literature. I. Title. II. Series.
  RC483.5.F55E84 2007
  616.85'27061—dc22
                                    2006006592

Interior design by MK Bassett-Harvey.
Interiors produced by Harding House Publishing Service, Inc.
www.hardinghousepages.com.
Cover design by Peter Culatta.
Printed in the Hashemite Kingdom of Jordan.

This book is meant to educate and should not be used as an alternative to appropriate medical care. Its creators have made every effort to ensure that the information presented is accurate—but it is not intended to substitute for the help and services of trained professionals.

# Contents

Introduction    6

1. The Drug that Changed Psychiatry    9

2. The Wonder Drug: How Prozac Works    31

3. Prozac Plus: Using Prozac with Other Therapies    47

4. Prozac Backlash    65

5. Prozac, Commercials, and Consumers:
How Drug Marketing Impacts Culture    79

6. Beyond Prozac: What's Next for Psychiatric Medications?    99


Further Reading    110

For More Information    111

Glossary    113

Bibliography    115

Index    117

Picture Credits    119

Biographies    120

# Introduction
## by Andrew M. Kleiman, M.D.

From ancient Greece through the twenty-first century, the experience of sadness and depression is one of the many that define humanity. As long as human beings have felt emotions, they have endured depression. Experienced by people from every race, socioeconomic class, age group, and culture, depression is an emotional and physical experience that millions of people suffer each day. Despite being described in literature and music; examined by countless scientists, philosophers, and thinkers; and studied and treated for centuries, depression continues to remain as complex and mysterious as ever.

In today's Western culture, hearing about depression and treatments for depression is common. Adolescents in particular are bombarded with information, warnings, recommendations, and suggestions. It is critical that adolescents and young people have an understanding of depression and its impact on an individual's psychological and physical health, as well as the treatment options available to help those who suffer from depression.

Why? Because depression can lead to poor school performance, isolation from family and friends, alcohol and drug abuse, and even suicide. This doesn't have to be the case, since many useful and promising treatments exist to relieve the suffering of those with depression. Treatments for depression may also pose certain risks, however.

Since the beginning of civilization, people have been trying to alleviate the suffering of those with depression. Modern-day medicine and psychology have taken the understanding and treatment of depression to new heights. Despite their shortcomings, these treatments have helped millions and millions of people lead happier, more fulfilling and prosperous lives that would not be possible in generations past. These treatments, however, have their own risks, and for some people, may not be effective at all. Much work in neuroscience, medicine, and psychology needs to be done in the years to come.

Many adolescents experience depression, and this book series will help young people to recognize depression both in themselves and in those around them. It will give them the basic understanding of the history of depression and the various treatments that have been used to combat depression over the years. The books will also provide a basic scientific understanding of depression, and the many biological, psychological, and alternative treatments available to someone suffering from depression today.

Each person's brain and biology, life experiences, thoughts, and day-to-day situations are unique. Similarly, each individual experiences depression and sadness in a unique way. Each adolescent suffering from depression thus requires a distinct, individual treatment plan that best suits his or her needs. This series promises to be a vital resource for helping young people recognize and understand depression, and make informed and thoughtful decisions regarding treatment.

# Chapter 1

# *The Drug that Changed Psychiatry*

*I used to walk around with a black cloud over my head. . . . I was chronically depressed. That's how I felt about life; it was an abyss. But after taking Prozac®, my depression is simply gone. I'm not a different person, but I'm a better person.*
—Marie, 41, in *Making the Prozac Decision*

The first few days on [Prozac] I vomited a lot, and I got headaches. The Prozac doctor told me these were normal side effects in the early stages.

At first I didn't think much of the stuff. I was as obsessive as ever, needing to touch, tap, knock, and count my way through the day. I did notice I was sleeping a little better, although my dreams were jagged and relentless, filled with images of tide pools and the sounds of shouts.

And then one morning, about five days after I'd first started the drug, I opened my eyes at eight A.M. I'd turned out my light at midnight, which meant I'd gotten, for the first time in many months, a seamless eight hours of sleep. It was a Saturday, and stripes of sun were on my walls. I sat up.

Something was different. I looked at my hand. It was the same hand. I touched my face—nose, cheeks, chin, all there. I rubbed my eyes and went into the kitchen.

The kitchen, too, was the same—table, two pine chairs, gray linoleum buckled and cracked along the floor. The sink still dripped. The grass moved against my window ledge. All the same, all different. What was it?

It was as though I'd been visited by a blind piano tuner who had crept into my apartment at night, who had tweaked the ivory bones of my body, the taut strings in my skull, and now, when I pressed on myself, the same notes but with a mellower, fuller sound sprang out.
—Lauren Slater, 26, in *Prozac Diary*

When I was about thirteen years old, maybe fourteen, I felt pretty depressed. Life was hard and I didn't see a way out. Things in school were getting to me. Kids were getting to me. I felt different, like I didn't fit in. And sometimes I felt like I didn't want to live any more. My parents made me

## The Drug that Changed Psychiatry 11

see a counselor, and that helped some, but everything still seemed bad. So my doctor put me on Prozac.

I started taking it, and in a few days it worked great. I felt better. I started feeling like my old self again. But after about three months, it didn't seem to help anymore. I was back to where I started.

Yeah, Prozac worked fine. I guess it's great. But only for the short term.

—Dan, 22, college student

These three comments from real people who experienced varying degrees of depressive or obsessive symptoms illustrate why Prozac became the "wonder drug" of the late twentieth

*For many people, Prozac truly seems like a wonder drug.*

## Drug Approval

*Before a drug can be marketed in the United States, it must be officially approved by the Food and Drug Administration (FDA). Today's FDA is the primary consumer protection agency in the United States. Operating under the authority given it by the government, and guided by laws established throughout the twentieth century, the FDA has established a rigorous drug approval process that verifies the safety, effectiveness, and accuracy of labeling for any drug marketed in the United States.*

*While the United States has the FDA for the approval and regulation of drugs and medical devices, Canada has a similar organization called the Therapeutic Product Directorate (TPD). The TPD is a division of Health Canada, the Canadian government department of health. The TPD regulates drugs, medical devises, disinfectants, and sanitizers with disinfectant claims. Some of the things that the TPD monitors are quality, effectiveness, and safety. Just as the FDA must approve new drugs in the United States, the TPD must approve new drugs in Canada before those drugs can enter the market.*

century. Here was a drug that, for the first time in history, was easy to take, was not addictive, and was not fatal in high doses if a person overdosed. Not only did Prozac help people snap out of their depressions, reduce the number and severity of their obsessive behaviors, and improve their mood, it did so without doing long-term harm.

# The Drug that Changed Psychiatry

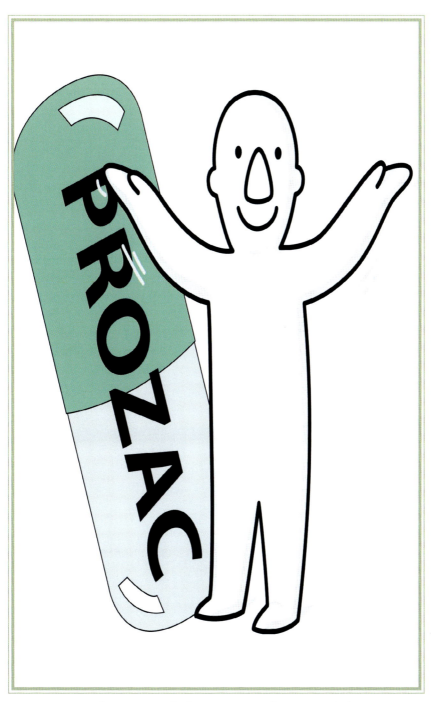

*Prozac revolutionized the way people viewed depression.*

## Prozac at a Glance

- brand names: *Prozac, Prozac Weekly, Sarafem*
- chemical name: *fluoxetine hydrochloride*
- drug class: *SSRI (selective serotonin reuptake inhibitor)*
- how it works: *blocks the reuptake of serotonin by presynaptic neurons*
- approved uses: *major depressive disorder; depressive disorder; obsessive-compulsive disorder (OCD); bulimia nervosa (binge eating and vomiting); panic disorders; premenstrual dysphoric disorder (PMDD)*
- habit forming? *no (although stopping medication suddenly can cause withdrawal symptoms)*
- available over-the-counter? *no*
- available by prescription? *yes*
- available as a generic? *yes, in some forms*
- how long until effect is noticeable? *one to four weeks*
- usual course of treatment: *six months to one year*
- common side effects: *dry mouth; fatigue; headache; nausea; decreased appetite; unusual weakness; constipation or diarrhea; inability to sleep; changes in sexual desire or ability; weight loss or weight gain*
- serious or potentially life-threatening side effects: *rash or hives; itchy skin; breathing difficulties; feelings of agitation; shaking or trembling; fever; joint pain; chest pain*
- warnings: *Do not take SSRIs if you currently take (or have taken in the last two weeks) an MAOI-class antidepressant (monoamine oxidase inhibitor; trade names Marplan, Nardil, Eldepryl, Parnate, etc.)*

## The Drug that Changed Psychiatry 15

The drug worked, and it didn't kill people. No wonder it skyrocketed to fame.

After Prozac's approval by the U.S. Food and Drug Administration (FDA) in 1987, the new antidepressant enjoyed nearly universal endorsement. Doctors valued the drug's low risk of side effects and complications. Patients raved that after months or years of depression, a few short weeks on Prozac made them feel normal again. People with depressive or anxiety disorders, some of whom had been in treatment for

*Many people who had suffered from anxiety and depression for years experienced relief for the first time when they used Prozac.*

> ### Brand Name vs. Generic Name
> 
> *Talking about psychiatric drugs can be confusing, because every drug has at least two names: its "generic name" and the "brand name" that the pharmaceutical company uses to market the drug. Generic names come from the drugs' chemical structure, while drug companies use brand names in order to inspire public recognition and loyalty for their product*

years, got well. Some even reported feeling "better than well," a phrase coined by psychiatrist and author Peter D. Kramer in *Listening to Prozac* and in the dozens of columns he wrote about Prozac for a psychiatric journal in the late 1980s and early 1990s.

As word spread about Prozac's success, the little green-and-cream-colored capsule became famous: it enjoyed two cover stories in *Newsweek* in less than four years, others in *Time* and the *New Yorker*, lead story status on *Nightline* and the *Today* show, celebrity endorsements, and widespread media reports. As a result, Prozac became the most widely known and readily accepted antidepressant in history. In fact, *Newsweek*'s initial cover image of a floating Prozac capsule represented the first time the magazine had run a cover image of any prescription drug.

Prozac's popularity was changing the faces of psychiatry, mental illness, and health care in general.

## Prozac and Psychiatry: Good News and Bad

"Prozac revolutionized modern psychiatric treatment," states Karl Benzio, a practicing psychiatrist and director of Lighthouse Education and Resource Network, a nonprofit foundation specializing in mental health education and training. In recent interviews, he described why and how Prozac changed psychiatry.

*Unfortunately, Prozac brought with it not only good news but bad as well.*

Previous psychiatric medications caused serious side effects, so for a patient to be put on these medications, his symptoms had to be quite severe. Even then, if a person's symptoms were serious enough to warrant the risks of taking dangerous psychiatric medications, often the dosages prescribed weren't high enough; psychiatrists didn't want to risk the damage higher doses of these medications could cause. This practice of avoiding side effects by maintaining low dosages made earlier psychiatric treatment attempts largely incomplete and unsuccessful. And even if lower doses of these medications seemed to work, as soon as patients exhibited improved symptoms doctors took them off these medications to avoid their most dangerous adverse effects.

Prozac and the newer SSRIs changed all that. With their low risk of side effects, doctors could safely keep most patients on these antidepressants for longer periods of time. Longer treatment gave psychiatrists the opportunity to help patients get through their crises and, once through them, to begin work on their underlying psychological needs. Prozac allowed psychiatrists to get at the root of a patient's issues—to examine their **psychodynamics**, if you will—while the patient was in a better, more healthy condition to do so.

Because Prozac helped people without apparently hurting them, psychiatrists were quick to prescribe the new drug. It wasn't that psychiatrists saw Prozac as a quick fix; in fact, just the opposite is true. Psychiatrists saw Prozac and the other selective serotonin reuptake inhibitors (SSRIs) as enabling their patients to become well enough to try supplemental strategies, including talk therapy, **behavioral therapy, cognitive therapy**, exercise, diet modification, and others. They

# The Drug that Changed Psychiatry

Prozac allowed psychiatrists and their patients to address complicated emotional issues.

viewed the drug as a tool in their psychiatric treatment boxes, but only a tool, and one to be used with other nondrug therapies.

Not all doctors felt the same way.

Dr. Benzio explains:

> When psychiatric medications held more complicated **nuances**, as the older ones did, they were left to psychiatrists to prescribe. But since the advent of safer meds, family practitioners who weren't as well-versed in other therapies and psychodynamics began writing more scripts [prescriptions]. Now patients could take the drug without pursuing additional therapies. And many began to view the SSRIs as miracle cures.
>
> The same is true today. Considering the psychiatric inexperience of many prescribing doctors along with the practices of America's managed-care health care system (the same one that limits how much time patients spend with doctors each visit and how many times patients can see doctors per year), it's easy to see why so little psychodynamic investigation happens for the average patient. Those who are depressed or obsessive today look to medication alone to solve their psychiatric issues. Talk therapy or cognitive therapy or behavioral therapy just isn't a high priority when insurance companies won't pay. So they rely on drugs alone.

What used to take years of psychodynamic investigation has now become a matter of seeing a family doctor and getting a script. For some people with depression, the easy approach of using drug treatment alone may work for the short term. For others, it won't work at all. Each case is different and needs to be evaluated individually. Unfortunately many family doctors don't have the time or the expertise, so they rely heavily on the medication route. And this "quick fix" attitude isn't an American phenomenon born only of American fast-paced culture, nor is it isolated to Western nations with Western ideals. It's a problem worldwide.

## Depression, Prozac, and the World

According to the World Health Organization (WHO), 25 percent of all individuals across the globe develop one or more

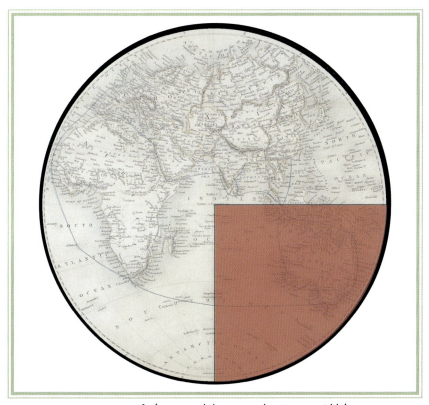

*One-quarter of the world's population will have a mental disorder at some point in their lives.*

## Accidental Discoveries: Prozac's Development Time Line

*1949:* Australian physician John Frederick Joseph Cade stumbles upon Lithium's effectiveness in treating bipolar disorders.

*1952:* Surgeon Dr. Henri Laborit, searching for a better anesthesia, notices the connection between antihistamines and calming effects in patients.

*1953:* Doctors discover that iproniazid, a drug used for treating tuberculosis, can help people with depression.

*1957:* Iproniazid is pulled off the market because of toxic side effects.

*1950s (late):* The first tricyclic antidepressants help depressed patients.

*1972:* Dr. David Wong of Eli Lilly makes preliminary discoveries about fluoxetine's ability to target only one neurotransmitter: serotonin.

*1976:* Eli Lilly begins trying fluoxetine on human patients.

*1982:* Zelmid®, the first SSRI, is introduced in Europe with great success.

*1983:* Officials pull Zelmid off the market because of dangerous side effects, including paralysis.

*1983:* Eli Lilly applies for FDA approval of fluoxetine (Prozac) for use in treating depression.

*1986:* Belgian officials approve Prozac for use in Belgium.

*1987:* The FDA approves fluoxetine for use in the United States.

*1988:* Prozac goes public.

*1989:* Prozac sales in the United States reach $350 million.

mental or behavioral disorders sometime in life, regardless of where they live. Of these, the leading mental disorder is depression. WHO estimates that 121 million (as of early 2006) have a depressive disorder, and that depression (along with **schizophrenia**) is a leading cause of suicide worldwide. How do treatment providers around the world handle this mental health crisis? The same as American treatment providers: They prescribe psychiatric drugs.

WHO concedes that the "first-line treatment" for those with depression is antidepressant medication. Practitioners in many countries, particularly developing nations, aren't trained in counseling, **psychotherapy**, or other listening therapies. With too few doctors available for too many patients, doctors often only have the time or resources to offer medication, nothing more. While this strategy may work for some, it's not how the developers of Prozac and other SSRIs intended them to be used.

## Prozac and the SSRIs: Where They Came From and How They Were Meant to Be Used

The story of Prozac's development begins quite by accident. In the early 1950s, a French surgeon, Henri Laborit, grew concerned over complications he saw in patients recovering from surgery: in particular, a significant drop in blood pressure and **postoperative shock**. The doctor believed the anesthesia used in surgery caused these symptoms, so if he could reduce the amount of anesthesia used, he should be able to lessen his patient's troubling symptoms. He began experimenting with antiallergy medications called antihistamines, known to induce sleep.

Dr. Laborit discovered that antihistamines not only reduced his patients' postoperative symptoms, but made the patients calmer before surgery, too. When the enterprising young physician told a colleague of his surprising results, that colleague told his brother-in-law, Pierre Deniker, who happened to be a psychiatrist. *If Laborit's drugs could calm surgical patients nervous about undergoing the scalpel,* Dr. Deniker reasoned, *then they might also calm psychiatric patients with agitation,*

*Before the invention of new drugs, patients with tuberculosis were treated with regimens of sunlight and fresh air.*

**manic** *moods, nervousness, and anxiety.* Dr. Deniker and his colleague, Jean Delay, administered chlorpromazine, one of the antihistamines Dr. Laborit used on surgical patients, to several long-term patients with mental illness institutionalized at Paris's St. Anne's Psychiatric Hospital. The drug worked. It eased the psychiatric patients' extreme emotions.

News of the doctors' success traveled quickly. By 1955, doctors in America were treating thousands of psychiatric patients with chlorpromazine, also recognized by its American trade name Thorazine®. Doctors now realized drugs could successfully impact the brain and the mind; chemicals, not just psychotherapy, could help the mentally ill. This breakthrough paved the way for the next accident leading to Prozac's discovery.

To lessen the growing threat of tuberculosis (TB), which claimed the lives of one out of every two victims, American doctors in 1953 began using a drug called iproniazid. Though the drug treated the lung disease effectively, practitioners noticed something else: TB patients who took iproniazid experienced improved appetites, increased energy levels, and overall feelings of well-being. Psychiatrists learned of these positive side effects on TB patients and began giving iproniazid to depressed patients, who by very nature of their depressive illnesses had little appetite, low energy levels, and feelings of despair. To the psychiatrists' amazement, the TB drug worked! Within the next year doctors used the "antidepressant" to treat over 400,000 people with depression and many responded well with treatment.

Though doctors in the 1950s didn't know *how* chlorpromazine or iproniazid worked, they knew these drugs did work—and with amazing results—on people's psyches. And though iproniazid's success didn't last long (it was pulled from the market because of toxic side effects), these early trials opened the door for what would become a flood of antidepressant drug discoveries.

First came the monoamine oxidase inhibitors (MAOIs), the first of which is iproniazid. MAOIs work by stopping a brain enzyme called monoamine oxidase from destroying other brain chemicals that affect mood, especially positive mood; they inhibit the action of monoamine oxidase. By keeping monoamine oxidase from killing off happiness-causing chemicals, more of these chemicals remain in the brain. And with more of these chemicals in the brain, a person seems better.

Then came the tricyclic antidepressants (TCAs). Like the MAOIs, TCAs affected brain chemicals. In fact, both drugs impacted several chemicals in the brain, not just one. And that was their problem. Because they affected so many brain chemicals, people who took them experienced unpleasant, unintended side effects: drowsiness, dry mouth, rapid heart rate, nausea, and constipation (among others), the most dangerous of which involved the heart and high blood pressure. Despite these unpleasantries, TCAs and MAOIs became the drugs of choice for treating depression for the next thirty years.

If only doctors could discover a drug that worked on only *one* brain chemical.

## The Drug that Changed Psychiatry

### A "Miracle" Is Found

By the late 1970s, drug developers had improved their understanding of how drugs impact the brain, especially how they affect the chemicals we now call "neurotransmitters." One of the lead researchers in the field at that time was Swedish pharmacologist Arvid Carlsson, the discoverer of the neurotransmitter called dopamine. Dr. Carlsson tested how different drugs affected various neurotransmitters. Like his French predecessor Dr. Laborit, Dr. Carlsson used antihistamines in

*In the 1970s, scientists discovered that certain chemicals had special impact on brain cells.*

his experiments. Trying an antihistamine called brompheniramine, the Swedish researcher observed how this drug impacted the reuptake of only two neurotransmitters: norepinephrine and serotonin. With these encouraging results, Dr. Carlsson and his colleagues sought to alter this drug to see if they could reduce its impact from two neurotransmitters to only one. They succeeded.

This new drug, named zimelidine, blocked only the reuptake of serotonin, nothing else. (Thus, when reuptake was blocked, more serotonin was left in the synapses, which helped improve mood.) It was the first drug to impact only one neurotransmitter. In fact, zimelidine was technically the first SSRI introduced to the world. Zimelidine, called by its trade name Zelmid®, became the number-one choice for treating depression in Europe in 1982; the U.S. and Canadian governments had not yet approved this drug's use in North America.

Shortly after Zelmid's European debut, people taking the new SSRI started getting sick. Some even died. Doctors learned that this drug, though effective in treating depression, could also cause a rare but sometimes fatal form of paralysis, Guillain-Barré syndrome. Because of this dangerous possibility, European officials pulled zimelidine off the market.

Meanwhile, across the Atlantic, American researchers at Eli Lilly, the Indiana-based pharmaceutical giant, researched antihistamines, too. In 1972 (ten years before the disaster with Zelmid), Eli Lilly researcher Dr. David Wong noticed that Lilly experimental drug number 110140 strongly inhibited the neurotransmitter serotonin, but barely inhibited norepinephrine, the only other neurotransmitter this drug affected. This drug, fluoxetine, would become the wildly popular drug we call Prozac today. But it took nearly fifteen additional years of research and human trials before the FDA approved fluoxetine for treating depression. The FDA issued its approval of Prozac on December 29, 1987.

Since then, the FDA and Prozac's manufacturer, Eli Lilly, have continued to investigate and monitor the drug. In fact, according to the FDA, Prozac had undergone over *fifty* labeling revisions in the years since its approval: everything from new warnings on packaging to new adverse events to new targeted patients, to new or modified indications for how the drug is to be used.

Like all prescription drugs, Prozac benefits certain people, but no drug is completely safe. Antidepressants, in particular, can impact the brain in predicted and unpredicted ways. To understand why this impact might be helpful (or unsafe) we first have to understand how these drugs work.

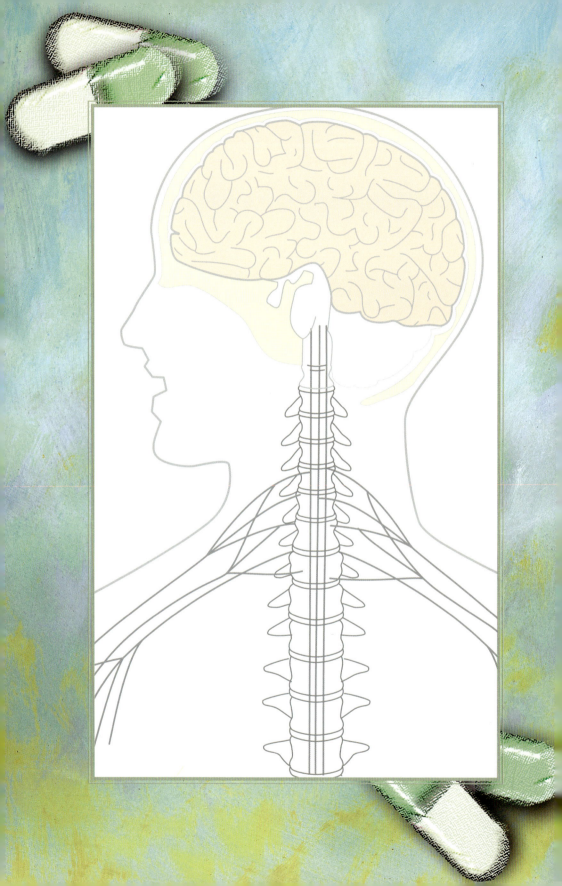

# Chapter 2

# *The Wonder Drug: How Prozac Works*

When Jacqueline woke each morning she both dreaded and looked forward to what came next: The Routine. The Routine, as she named it, consisted of carefully folding the blankets back off of her satin-pajama-bottom-covered legs, then swinging her feet over the right side of her bed (always the right, never the left), and sitting upright on the bed's edge. Placing both hands palms down next to her hips, Jacqueline pushed herself up from her mattress, stood tall, took a deep breath, then walked fifteen evenly spaced steps to her bathroom sink (always fifteen, never fourteen or sixteen). There she brushed her teeth using twenty upward brush strokes and twenty

downward brush strokes (no more, no less) on every section of her mouth. She then rinsed her mouth for twenty seconds, rinsed again, and then rinsed one more time for her usual habit of three rinses each morning, twenty seconds each. And that was just the beginning of The Routine.

Next came her shower. Carefully disrobing and stepping into the shower, Jacqueline made sure to place her feet on the exact spots on the shower floor she'd marked for them; she didn't dare place her feet incorrectly or she'd have to start The Routine over again. Once her feet found their spots, the repetitions began in Jacqueline's mind: *one, two, three, four . . . eighteen, nineteen, twenty scrubs for my right arm. There. Now, one, two, three, four . . . eighteen, nineteen, twenty scrubs for my left.* Over and over again Jacqueline repeated her twenty scrubs for every part of her body. If she lost count or forgot where she'd already washed, she started again with her right arm: *one, two, three. . . .*

The repetition and routine helped Jacqueline feel secure; it gave her a sense of power and control. And though The Routine could take three hours or more on some mornings, the sacrifice seemed worth it. Completing The Routine perfectly gave Jacqueline great satisfaction.

But it frightened her, too. Especially since The Routine had become increasingly demanding. First it had only involved counting the steps to the bathroom and brushing her teeth with ten upward and downward strokes. Then it demanded exact foot placement on the shower floor. Then the twenty-scrub routine. What was next?

# The Wonder Drug: How Prozac Works 33

Jacqueline realized The Routine, something she once controlled, now controlled her.

What was wrong?

What Jacqueline, the fictional teenager in this opening scenario, didn't realize is that her compulsive behavior comes from a problem in her brain, more specifically from a problem in the way her brain's nerve cells, called neurons, communicate with each other.

## Communication in the Brain: Like Central Command

Billions of neurons make up the brain, and they communicate with each other to relay messages from one part of the brain

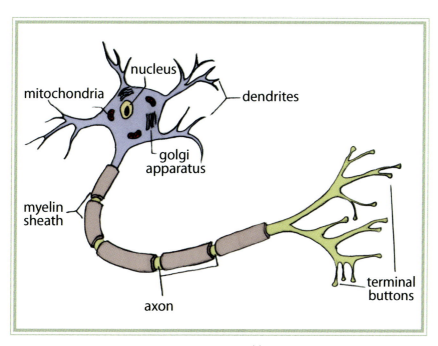

*A nerve cell*

to the next, and ultimately to the rest of the body. Let's say for example, another fictional teenager, José Luis, wants to move his right hand. The motor part of José's brain, the section controlling body movements, needs to send a message to the muscles in José's right hand that it's time for them to contract. But sending this message requires a complicated coordination of events to get each muscle to contract at the appropriate time and in the right sequence for José to move his hand the way he wants to.

*The brain is the body's Central Command that telephones messages to the rest of the body.*

To ensure that the proper combination of messages is sent at the right time to the right places, the brain serves as the body's command post. In this sense, the brain acts like a military's Central Command. Central Command controls all military movements; it coordinates the actions of various forces under its command. If one unit comes under enemy fire, Central Command receives news of the attack, checks the location of other forces that might help the barraged unit, and then sends reinforcements. Coordinating which troops are where and how they interact requires detailed communication between Central Command and its troops.

The troops, however, can't know what to do unless they receive Central Command's messages. In the same way, the muscles in José's hand won't know how and when to move unless they receive the messages from his brain.

To send messages, the brain uses neurons. Unlike a military command center that uses one messenger to carry a message, the brain uses billions of these nerve cells working together, much like a bucket brigade does when passing water buckets from a water source to a fire: it passes the message from one neuron to the next until the message reaches its final destination, in this case, José's hand.

This process may sound easy enough, but much can go wrong. If you think of a bucket brigade again, many things can happen to prevent the filled water bucket from reaching the fire. First, the bucket might not be filled completely. Next, the person filling the bucket might not pass the bucket well (may drop it or slosh the water out of the bucket while

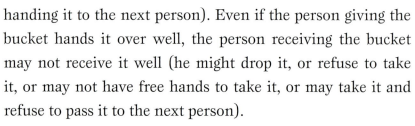

handing it to the next person). Even if the person giving the bucket hands it over well, the person receiving the bucket may not receive it well (he might drop it, or refuse to take it, or may not have free hands to take it, or may take it and refuse to pass it to the next person).

A similar chain of events happens between nerve cells: you need a sending person (a person with the filled bucket who is giving the bucket away); you need a means to carry the water (the pail); and you need a receiving person (the person who will receive the bucket when it's given to him). In the brain's "brigade," the sending cells are called presynaptic neurons; the pails (the message carriers) are chemical agents called neurotransmitters; the receiving cells are the postsynaptic neurons. The space between the sending cell and the receiving cell is called the synapse.

When José's brain decides it's time for his hand to move, here's what happens. The message originates in a presynaptic (before-the-space) neuron and travels through that neuron's **axon** to the terminal buttons at its axon's end. There, the terminal buttons hand the message to the chemical message carriers (the neurotransmitters) that, in turn, carry the message across the synapse to the postsynaptic (after-the-space) neuron. The postsynaptic neuron receives the message through its message receptors (called dendrites, which are the equivalent of a bucket-brigade person's hand). The message travels through the receiving cell's dendrites into that cell, where it crosses to its cell's other end. When it reaches the opposite end of the cell, the message passes through that cell's axon to the sending centers at its end. That neuron, the one that originally received the message, has now processed the message and is sending it to the next cell. In effect, the postsynaptic neuron (the receiving cell) has become a presynaptic neuron (the sending cell), just as a member of a bucket brigade receives the pail of water, passes it to his other hand, then hands the pail onto the next person.

Like the bucket brigade, the brain's communication system can break down.

## Communication Problems

Researchers now link depression and many other psychiatric disorders to the part of the brain's communication system called neurotransmitters, the chemical message carriers serving like pails in a bucket brigade. Sometimes the sending cell

*Messages are passed along between nerve cells, with neurotransmitters like serotonin acting as the "buckets."*

does the equivalent of handing too many pails to the next cell at one time for the receiving cell to take them all; sometimes the sending cell sends just enough, but the receiving cell's hands are full and can't take the pails handed to it; sometimes the receiving cell isn't fast enough, so the sending cell takes its pails back (called reuptake); and sometimes the brain just doesn't have enough pails (enough of certain chemicals). As a result, the brain ends up with either too many pails (too

*When the brain lacks enough neurotransmitters to pass messages, it's as though it had too few "buckets" to carry the message.*

much of a neurotransmitter) or too few pails (too little of a neurotransmitter).

While researchers have identified hundreds of neurotransmitters in the human body, dozens of which carry messages in the human brain, they believe the neurotransmitter serotonin is most responsible for various forms of depression. In effect, when the brain has too little serotonin floating in the synapses between its neurons, a person can develop depressive symptoms. One way to increase the amount of serotonin is to keep the sending cells from taking back the serotonin leftovers—to inhibit serotonin reuptake.

As Prozac prevented neurons from taking back excess serotonin found in the synapse, the overall levels of serotonin in the synapse increased. As researchers discovered, when these levels of serotonin increased, over time, so did the person's sense of well-being. Researchers had found an effective treatment for serotonin-shortage-caused depression.

But while increased serotonin levels can be a good thing, too much could cause problems.

## Serotonin Storm

While on vacation in the mountains, sixteen-year-old Adam begged his father, Doug, to let him drive the four-wheel all-terrain-vehicle (ATV) on the back-country roads they'd been navigating together (with Doug driving) all afternoon. After much pleading on Adam's part, Doug relented and allowed Adam to take the handlebars. Adam revved the motor while his nervous dad climbed behind him to supervise his son's driving.

40    Prozac: North American Culture and the Wonder Drug

All went well until the pair crested a hill and began a long, winding descent over an old lumbering trail. As they accelerated, Doug yelled to Adam to slow down, but with his gaze fixed and hands clenched tight on the accelerator, the teen

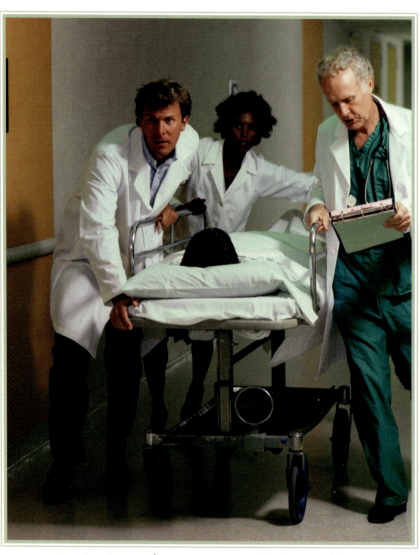

*Serotonin syndrome may require immediate emergency medical care.*

## Causes of Serotonin Syndrome

SSRI overdose
Interaction between an SSRI and other drugs or medications
Regular SSRI use (rarely)

## Symptoms of Serotonin Syndrome

confusion
irritability
diarrhea
muscle rigidity
high fever
chills
hot, dry skin
poor coordination
hallucinations
feeling drunk or dizzy
sweating
trembling or shaking
twitching
seizure
loss of consciousness

## What to do if you think you or a loved one has serotonin syndrome:

Seek emergency medical help and treatment immediately.

seemed to ignore his father. They accelerated even more. As the two approached a dangerous bend, Doug screamed at his son to stop, but Adam didn't respond. The force of the curve whipped the terrified father off the back of the ATV, while the ATV plowed forward out of control until it ran into construction pipes stacked in a gully next to the trail further down the road. The ATV exploded in flames, igniting Adam's jacket. His father, now running down the hill toward the accident scene, watched helplessly as his son writhed in pain.

So began an episode of the television drama *House.* The lead character, Dr. Gregory House, played by British actor Hugh Laurie, is a brilliant diagnostician specializing in infectious diseases. Though abrasive, rude, and possessing a terrible bedside manner, Dr. House receives only the most puzzling cases. His unconventional approaches and solid diagnostic instincts make him known as the doctor who can solve cases other doctors can't.

Initially thought to be a typical burn patient, Adam doesn't command Dr. House's attention until some of his tests come back with atypical results. Especially puzzling is the boy's irregular heartbeat. His symptoms don't fit the typical burn patient. Enter Dr. House.

After much drama and investigation, Dr. House and his team suspect Adam may be suffering from a condition known as "serotonin storm." This condition was the cause of his accident, and the symptoms of this condition are complicating his recovery.

A decade ago, physicians had barely heard of this diagnosis, let alone people within the television industry. The diagnosis'

# The Wonder Drug: How Prozac Works 43

*When the brain is overwhelmed with serotonin, it can trigger a physical crisis.*

mention on *House* in 2006 indicates just how far doctors and the public have come in their understanding of serotonin and its impact on the brain. It never would have been mentioned on this program otherwise.

To explain serotonin storm (or serotonin syndrome as it is also called), researchers suggest that as patients lower their SSRI dosages the brain's natural serotonin-producing system

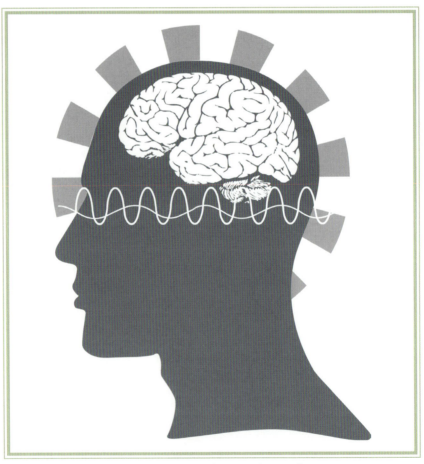

*The brain is a complicated mechanism whose workings can be upset.*

might kick into overdrive, flooding the brain with too much serotonin—causing a literal storm of serotonin in the brain. Patients begin to experience dizziness or lightheadedness, nausea, vomiting, headaches, lethargy, sweating, insomnia, anxiety, agitation, twitching, and panic. They can also develop seizures, as Adam did in the *House* episode (which was what caused his ATV accident).

Too much serotonin can also occur when SSRI dosages are too high, when dosages are increased too rapidly, or when SSRIs interact with other medications. Thankfully, serotonin storm can be successfully treated when correctly diagnosed.

Despite their risks and documented adverse effects, SSRIs help hundreds of thousands of people each year without causing long-term health problems. Doctors, however (especially psychiatrists), are learning that SSRIs alone don't provide the long-term solution many people with depressive or anxiety disorders need. Studies show that when SSRIs (or other antidepressants) supplement other treatment strategies, patients experience the best, longest-lasting benefits.

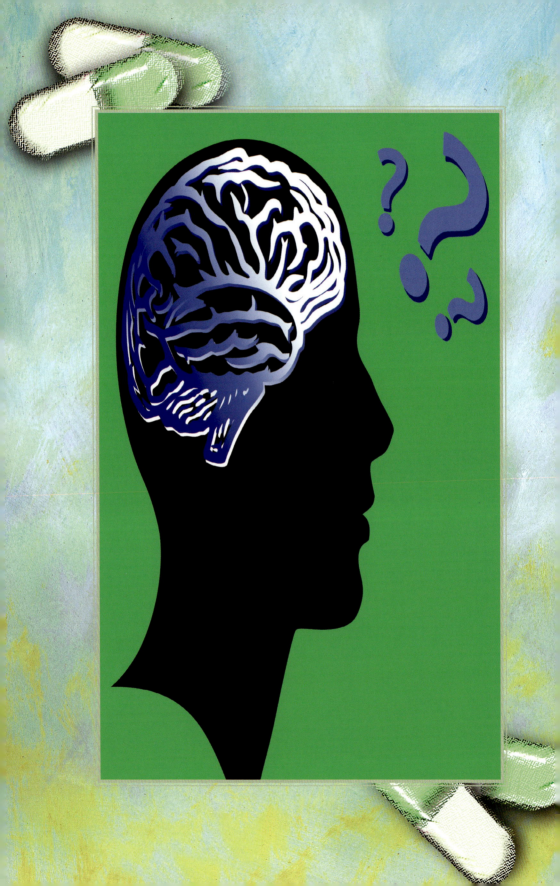

# Chapter 3

# *Prozac Plus: Using Prozac with Other Therapies*

Though Prozac has done much good and has even saved lives, it helps only 30 percent of those with severe, chronic depression. William S. Appleton, a private-practice psychiatrist for over thirty-five years, notes in his work *Prozac and the New Antidepressants* that Prozac's success rate is better when you count all types of depressive disorders (closer to 70 percent), but in no case is Prozac the cure-all or panacea many thought it was going to be when the drug first entered the market. As Dr. Appleton states, "it is not a miracle drug."

The most effective treatment for depressive or anxiety disorders is to use medications like SSRIs to supplement other treatment strategies. In the broadest terms, these other strategies can fall into two groups: those that involve treatment providers (people) and those that do not.

## Supplemental or Alternate Therapies Involving Treatment Providers

The first group, which involve the patient going to a healthcare provider, includes several options, the most common of which include cognitive therapy (addresses how a person thinks), behavioral therapy (addresses how a person acts), cognitive-behavioral therapy (CBT), talk therapy/counseling (allows a person to talk through his issues), psychodynamic investigation (looks at how a person's medical history, past experiences, psychological issues, and deep-rooted thoughts and emotions affect that person today; this strategy is also known as psychotherapy), and life coaching (helps a person make lifestyle changes to work toward healing). Other lesser-known approaches exist, but these six are the most common.

### Cognitive Therapy

"I can't believe I lost it the way I did," seventeen-year-old Marissa confided to her therapist. "I mean, it was such a stupid thing. One minute we were laughing and messing around and stuff, and the next I was crying. He just had to mention Nadine. I know she doesn't mean anything to him anymore, but I just couldn't help it."

"Why do you think his mentioning her upset you?" Marissa's therapist probed. "Do you remember what you were thinking?"

# Prozac Plus: Using Prozac with Other Therapies 49

*Our thoughts are powerful forces that shape our emotions and behaviors.*

"I guess . . . well, ah . . . I don't really know. Not any one thing and a thousand things. I'm not sure. I suppose I thought things like *she's prettier than me* and *he still loves her* and *he just wants me around because he can't have her* and *what I am doing thinking a guy like Jared could ever love a girl like me*. I don't know exactly. All I know is that one minute we were

*Cognitive therapy seeks to make individuals more aware of their thoughts, so that they can make their thought habits more positive.*

having fun, and then I was crying." Marissa looked at her therapist and fell silent.

"Let's look at some of your thoughts for a minute," suggested the psychologist. "Let's see how much of your thinking reflects what is true and how much has been influenced by your emotions and thought habits."

Marissa leaned forward and concentrated on her cognitive therapy session. It might not make her feel better instantly, but she knew it would show her how to think in ways that would help her be a happier person.

Cognitive therapy deals with the mind: with how an individual thinks, what an individual believes, and how an individual processes information. Cognitive therapy is especially important for those with depressive disorders because depression can affect how a person thinks.

For example, someone with depression may tend to think in all-or-nothing terms: always, never, hopeless, worthless. He might think something like *I'll never feel better,* when the reality is his feelings will pass. Or she may think *I always mess up,* when a more accurate thought would be *I sometimes make mistakes, just like everyone else, but I do things right a lot of the time, too.*

Cognitive therapy helps the individual learn to take charge of her thinking and to replace false thoughts with truth.

## Behavioral Therapy

Behavioral therapy works similarly to cognitive therapy in that it replaces something negative with something positive, only in this case, the individual replaces a behavior instead of a thought. When a person is trying to quit smoking, for example, instead of lighting up when he feels the urge to smoke, he might suck on a lollypop or chew gum. Or when someone is prone to angry outbursts, her therapist might suggest she leave the room or go for a jog or count to ten when she feels angry. If an individual is struggling with an addiction, his counselor may suggest that he replace old habits (hanging around bars or going to parties) with new behaviors (joining a gym or getting involved in a hobby). The idea is to replace the old behavior with something new and more beneficial. Behavioral therapists help their patients identify negative or self-destructive behaviors and then suggest positive behaviors their patients can use as replacements.

## Cognitive-Behavioral Therapy (CBT)

As its name implies, CBT involves both cognitive (thought) and behavioral (action) therapies. Therapists help patients identify the thoughts behind their actions, evaluate if the thoughts are accurate, learn to replace inaccurate thoughts with accurate ones, and then develop appropriate behaviors in response to their more accurate thinking.

## Talk Therapy/Counseling

In talk therapy, a person like Marissa might discuss her relationship with her boyfriend: what happened, how she felt, what she thought, how and why she felt that way. By talking through her issues, she can freely and safely express her thoughts and emotions and then work toward understanding herself better. While the therapist's job in talk therapy

## Prozac Plus: Using Prozac with Other Therapies

sessions is primarily to listen, he can also offer objective insight into his client's thoughts and behaviors, an angle on her circumstances and behaviors that the client herself can't see. The talk therapist or counselor can also provide counsel or advice, but usually only with the patient's permission or at the patient's request.

### Psychodynamic Investigation

Of the supplemental strategies, psychodynamic investigation is the most complicated and the one most often used by

*Psychodynamic investigation examines one's childhood relationships and experiences.*

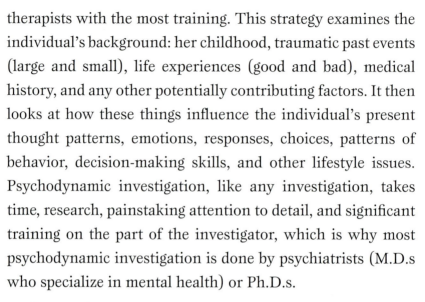

therapists with the most training. This strategy examines the individual's background: her childhood, traumatic past events (large and small), life experiences (good and bad), medical history, and any other potentially contributing factors. It then looks at how these things influence the individual's present thought patterns, emotions, responses, choices, patterns of behavior, decision-making skills, and other lifestyle issues. Psychodynamic investigation, like any investigation, takes time, research, painstaking attention to detail, and significant training on the part of the investigator, which is why most psychodynamic investigation is done by psychiatrists (M.D.s who specialize in mental health) or Ph.D.s.

## Life Coaching

If psychodynamic investigation is the most complicated of the supplemental strategies, life coaching is the least. One person, the coach, comes alongside another, the person-in-training, and helps him develop the skills he needs to live a productive, satisfying life. A life coach's role is much like that of an athletic coach: to challenge, cheer, equip, train, encourage, and mentor trainees into reaching their potentials. The life coach's responsibilities can include everything from providing encouragement over the phone, to offering advice, to providing specific strategies for dealing with various issues (career choice, conflicts at work, parenting—you name it, and there's undoubtedly a life coach somewhere providing it).

Life coaching, psychodynamic investigation, talk therapy, behavioral therapy, cognitive therapy, and CBT could fall under the loose umbrella of interpersonal or relational treatment strategies. They all involve an individual meeting with a treatment provider in one-on-one or group therapy sessions. Beyond these relationship-oriented strategies, someone with depression or anxiety can try nonrelational techniques to supplement their drug-treatment regimens.

*A life coach may offer specific strategies for dealing with finances, career choices, or other life issues.*

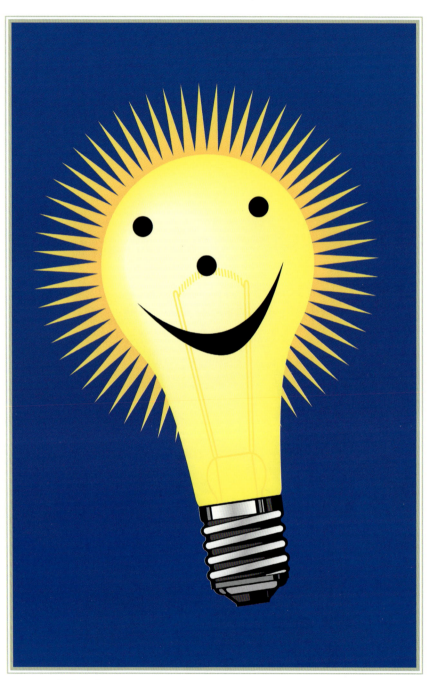

*Light therapy may increase a person's serotonin levels, thereby making her feel happier.*

## Supplemental or Alternative Strategies: No Additional People Necessary

Not all therapies involve treatment providers. Many people with depression and anxiety issues find relief from their symptoms using these techniques:

### Light Therapy

Researchers have long known that light affects mental outlook. Most people, in fact, feel more energetic on bright, sunny days and less energetic on dark, dreary days. It wasn't until the mid- to late- twentieth century, however, that scientists began to understand why. Light, they theorized, impacts our moods and energy levels because it impacts the amount of serotonin in our brains: the more light a person is exposed to, the higher her serotonin levels will be; the less light she receives, the lower her serotonin levels will be. If low serotonin levels make us feel depressed and lethargic, and low serotonin levels result from less exposure to light, then increased exposure to light should improve our mood. This is the reasoning behind light therapy.

Light therapy, also called phototherapy, involves the use of a special light in front of which the patient sits for various lengths of time. This light is not an ordinary light like those found in the common home; it's much brighter, much more intense, and includes the full spectrum of light rays. It also includes a special filter to protect the patient's eyes from damaging rays included in the light spectrum.

When used correctly, light therapy helps 75 percent of people with seasonal affective disorder (SAD), a form of seasonal depression, even without drug therapy. People with other depressive illnesses find relief from their symptoms using light therapy in addition to drug treatment.

## Diet and Exercise

According to exercise physiologists, sustained aerobic exercise increases serotonin levels, too. Even without drug intervention, exercise can increase serotonin levels enough to effectively eliminate depressive feelings for someone with mild depression. That's why so many doctors encourage people

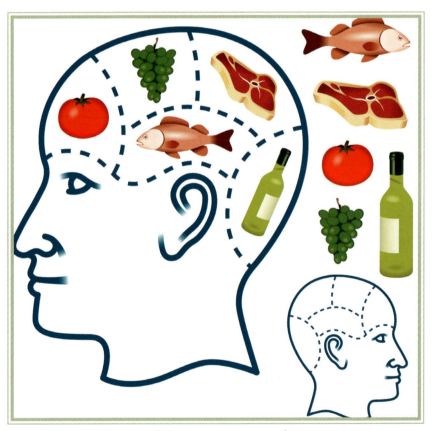

*In some ways it's true: you are what you eat!*

with depressed moods to get more exercise. Yoga and deep-breathing exercises have also been shown to improve mood.

Foods, nutritionists have discovered, impact metabolism as well. Caffeine in coffee, chocolate, and soda makes us feel alert (momentarily); sugar and other carbohydrates boost our energy; turkey makes us sleepy (think of post-Thanksgiving dinner naps). What we eat impacts how we feel. People with depressive tendencies often find some relief from their symptoms when they alter their eating habits to reflect a healthy balance of grains, fruits, vegetables, proteins, dairy products, and fats.

For some people, maintaining a healthy diet and a regular exercise routine is enough to overcome their mild depressions, even without medication-based treatment. For others, dietary and lifestyle changes won't be enough; they'll need medications to ultimately balance the chemicals in their brains.

## Faith-Based Activities (Prayer, Meditation, Church/Synagogue/Mosque Attendance)

Current research suggests faith may contribute to health and healing. American television network MSNBC launched a series of reports on this phenomenon in 2005, as did *Newsweek* magazine. One study quoted in both reports stated that people who attended church regularly outlived people who didn't—a nearly 25 percent difference in mortality rates. In his work *God, Faith, and Health,* Jeff Levin cites a Johns Hopkins study in which researchers found that monthly religious attendance more than halved a person's risk of death from heart disease,

> ## Mental Health Tips
>
> Try these seven non-drug tips for improving your mental health:
>
> Sunday: Relax (meditate, pray, walk outdoors, etc.).
>
> Monday: Make a plan (a to-do list: if too much is on it, cut something).
>
> Tuesday: Surround yourself with supportive people (family, friends).
>
> Wednesday: Take care of your body (exercise, eat right, sleep).
>
> Thursday: Give of yourself (volunteer, serve, help someone else).
>
> Friday: Broaden your horizons (try something new, vary your routine).
>
> Saturday: Value yourself (treat yourself).
>
> (Source: National Mental Health Association)

emphysema, cirrhosis of the liver, suicide, and some cancers. Though studies are still inconclusive, researchers suspect similar correlations between faith and recovery from (or prevention of) depressive illness.

The United States National Center for Health Statistics reported in 2004 that three out of every hundred people in America experienced significant psychological stress within thirty days of the survey, or roughly 3 percent of those questioned. That equals nearly 8.5 million people (based on the U.S. Census Bureau's population estimate of 281.4 million U.S. citizens for the year 2000). If faith helped just 1 percent of these individuals get through their psychological traumas (a low estimate by any standard), it could prevent 85,000 people from developing the full-blown depressive episodes normally associated with this kind of psychological stress.

Though not documented, the correlation between faith and wellness may have to do with faith's influence on a person's attitude toward the future. Those with depression often view the future with hopelessness and despair; people of faith, no matter what religion they follow, look at the future with hope and optimism. Hope is a powerful antidote to despair. Faith, then, though it hasn't been proven to change brain chemistry, can become an important weapon in the battle to overcome depressive illnesses.

## Alternate Chemical Substances (Herbs, Vitamins, Natural Remedies, etc.)

Before trying herbs or vitamins to supplement a drug treatment regimen for depression, remember this: *herbs and vitamins (and other supplements) are chemicals, just like their prescription counterparts.* They can and will affect the way you think, act, and feel, just as prescription drugs do. They can and will cause side effects, just like those that accompany prescription drugs. They can and will cause drug interactions, just like prescription drugs can. For these reasons, it's important to *always* consult with a physician before attempting to treat a psychological disorder with herbs or vitamins.

These four alternatives or supplements to drug therapy (light therapy, diet and exercise, faith-based activities, and alternate substances) are the most common strategies not requiring a therapist or counselor. Most therapists and counselors will recommend these supplemental strategies for treating

## Common Natural Remedies

*St. John's wort (Hypericum perforatum): for mild depression*

*black cohosh: to relieve symptoms of menopause and PMS*

*valerian: for sleep disturbances and insomnia*

*gingko: for memory problems or inability to concentrate*

*kava: for anxiety*

*chamomile: for tension headaches and anxiety*

## Common Side Effects of Natural Remedies

*St. John's wort: dry mouth, upset stomach, dizziness, diarrhea*

*black cohosh (rarely): stomach pain, intestinal upset, headaches*

*valerian: possible liver damage*

*gingko: upset stomach, dizziness, headaches, allergic reactions*

*kava (only in large doses): breathing difficulties, muscle spasms*

*chamomile (rarely): allergic reactions*

depression *in addition to* drug therapies. They realize Prozac and the other SSRIs (as well as other psychiatric drugs) work best when used together with other strategies including those requiring treatment providers and those that don't.

Even in the best of circumstances, however, Prozac (and other SSRIs) can fail or cause unintended problems. When first released, Prozac seemed like a miracle cure because little was known of its long-term side effects (no one had been on the drug long enough to see what happened). But as people took Prozac over longer periods of time, doctors and patients alike began to discover unexpected consequences of taking the drug, a phenomenon eventually termed "Prozac backlash."

# Chapter 4

## *Prozac Backlash*

*D*ialogue from a TeenHelp.org support forum:

*I've been diagnosed with dysthymia and would like to know if anyone else [with this diagnosis] went on Prozac and what their experience was. I'm really sitting on the fence about this. Part of me says "what have I got to lose?" and another part says, "I'm a failure and weak" if I do that. He (my therapist) has been pushing this for almost two years now, since I was diagnosed, but he believes it started around puberty. Any comments would be great! Thanks!*

Answers:
05-15-2005, 05:32 AM

*I took Prozac for depression and my body couldn't handle it. It all depends on you and your body.*

05-15-2005, 06:15 AM

*I was on Prozac for a few months and eventually got up to the maximum dosage, and it did nothing for me, really. If anything*

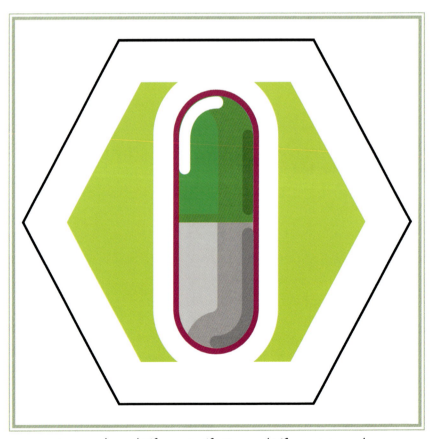

Prozac has different effects on different people.

*it made me more depressed/suicidal. If memory serves, most (if not all) of my attempts were while I was on Prozac. Don't get me wrong, it can and might work for you . . . it just depends on your chemistry. They put me on it because it did wonders for my mom . . . I guess thinking about our blood relations . . . but it was the opposite. Prescribing medicine, especially when there are so many different kinds for the same illness, is really difficult. In the end it is all trial and error. I'm on like number three or four.*

05-15-2005, 07:02 AM

*Well, my best friend was diagnosed with depression, and she got put on Prozac. It turned her reckless and mean. She didn't have any regard for what other people felt or anything. But now she's off it and I love her again.*

05-15-2005, 08:29 AM

*I take Prozac for depression. Prozac seemed to help for a while. It doesn't now. I think it's more that I've forgotten some doses than it's wearing off. But what do you have to lose? Your therapist should want to watch you very VERY carefully because Prozac can cause a rise in suicidal tendencies for a few weeks.*

05-15-2005, 11:54 AM

*I took it for just over a year and found everything to be slightly less harsh, but even at fairly high doses it was certainly no revelation (note I was taking it for OCD not depression).*

This brief dialogue, quoted from an online advice forum for teenagers, represents a variety of opinions about Prozac and the SSRI drug family. The good news, as we've seen in previous chapters, is these drugs really do help people, especially those with mild-to-moderate depressive and anxiety disorders. The bad news it this: Prozac and other SSRIs can lose their effectiveness and, worse, can cause serious (sometimes fatal) side effects.

> September 1989: Angry after being humiliated at work, forty-seven-year-old printing press operator Joseph Wesbecker went to his place of employment armed with an AK47, shot and killed eight coworkers, wounded twelve others, then turned the gun on himself. He'd been taking Prozac under a doctor's supervision for only a few weeks.

> March 1993: After being on Prozac for only eleven days, sixty-three-year-old William Forsyth stabbed his wife of thirty-seven years fifteen times with a serrated kitchen knife, and then impaled himself with the same blade. Both died.

> November 1997: Australian rock band INXS's lead vocalist, Michael Hutchence, hanged himself with his belt. Investigators found a bottle of Prozac in the room where he committed suicide.

> May 1998: Fifteen-year-old Oregon resident Kip Kinkel shot his parents one day and several of his Thurston High School classmates the next after being prescribed Prozac for depression.

> March 2005: Sixteen-year-old northern Minnesota high school student Jeff Weise shot and killed his grandfather, eight others, and then himself. A long-time friend reported that the teen had been on Prozac since his previous suicide attempt nine months earlier.

These represent some of the extreme cases where reporters, researchers, or other individuals claim Prozac caused personal violence and suicidal tendencies in patients taking the drug. However, keep in mind that these stories do not prove that Prozac is dangerous. It might be just as likely that the individuals in these cases were simply prescribed Prozac because of already existing emotional difficulties, the same difficulties that eventually caused them to become violent or suicidal.

*Prozac has plenty of critics!*

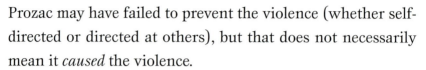

Prozac may have failed to prevent the violence (whether self-directed or directed at others), but that does not necessarily mean it *caused* the violence.

Other stories illustrate Prozac's better-documented and less serious effects. Author Joseph Glenmullen recounts his experience with a patient he identifies as "Maura":

> Late in therapy, Maura took to lying back in the chair in my office, so relaxed she looked as if she drifted into a peaceful, tranquil state as we spoke. . . . I would especially watch Maura's face at these times . . . her face was a study in repose.
>
> Unfortunately, this peace, hard won throughout a year of psychotherapy, was shattered by a chance observation on my part as I gazed at Maura's face. Suddenly I began to notice twitching all around her eyes. Her closed eyelids pressed more tightly shut. Waves of muscular contractions circled around her eyes. Bursts of this abnormal twitching punctuated periods of relative calm in which the muscles appeared to relax with just faint background activity.

This brief episode describes a lesser known, but documented side effect of antidepressants and other medications: facial tics, a form of dyskinesia (uncontrolled abnormal movements). Studies find that the most common medicine-related dyskinesias involve abnormal movements in the mouth, jaw, and tongue.

No one really knows where facial tics or other dyskinesias come from, only that they occur in response to taking some medications. Some researchers and physicians believe these and other documented side effects from Prozac and the

SSRIs may come from an unintended consequence in the brain. Though Prozac's action causes the ultimate increase of the brain's serotonin (its desired effect), the desired increase apparently causes the brain to produce less of a second

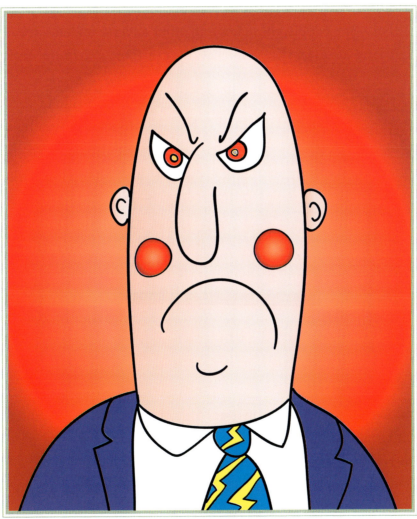

*Prozac may not eliminate an individual's tendency to rage and violence—but that does not mean that Prozac caused that tendency.*

neurotransmitter, dopamine, by as much as 50 percent. Researchers call this corresponding drop in dopamine a backlash: a strong reaction by the brain to the increased serotonin levels. They believe Prozac backlash is responsible for the SSRIs' most severe neurological side effects, including facial tics.

For some people, these tics and other adverse effects appear not long after starting medication and then **dissipate** until they finally disappear on their own. For others they worsen. For a few, they become permanent, even after the patient stops taking the medication that initially caused the problem. In Maura's case, though Dr. Glenmullen pulled Maura off Prozac a week after he first noticed her dyskinesia, her facial tics worsened in the following weeks and months. Two weeks after taking her last dose of Prozac, Maura called Dr. Glenmullen and said, "Something dreadful is happening to me. . . . I need to see a neurologist. My lips are twitching and my tongue keeps darting out of my head." The doctor agreed to see her right away, and recounts his observations.

> **Prozac's Most Common Side Effects:**
>
> lessened sexual desire
>
> inability to reach orgasm
>
> memory problems
>
> headache
>
> dry mouth

When [Maura] came, I was flabbergasted. . . . Her lips now displayed twitching similar to that which I had observed around her eyes. But worst of all was the tongue-darting: fly-catcher-type movements in which her curled tongue darted in and out. The tongue-darting together with the twitching was disfiguring.

Maura's symptoms continued to worsen until she finally avoided being seen in public. Her facial tics were so obvious and disfiguring she wouldn't go out unless she wore scarves and sunglasses. Two months after stopping Prozac, her facial

A headache is one of the most common side effects of Prozac.

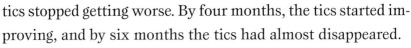

tics stopped getting worse. By four months, the tics started improving, and by six months the tics had almost disappeared.

Maura is only one case, but she represents thousands of antidepressant takers who experienced similar reactions to their medications. While information about these frightening and sometimes dangerous side effects initially appeared in early documentation, most didn't come to light until years after Prozac's public debut.

In recent years drug regulators made startling discoveries, the most disturbing of which was that some antidepressant manufacturers knew of these horrible side effects before they offered their drugs to the public. Drug developers observed these events in pre-approval **clinical trials** required by the FDA, but they failed to notify regulators or the public of their severity.

After taking the drug companies to court, officials successfully gained access to previously hidden drug company records, finally seeing for themselves *all* that happened in various clinical trials. These documents recorded episodes of severe agitation, self-harm, aggression, and suicidal behaviors in people taking the drugs being tested, especially those taking SSRIs. Sometimes the behaviors worsened as dosages increased; other times the behaviors appeared only when the subjects reduced their dosages. The observed agitation and suicidal tendencies consistently affected adolescents and young adults more extremely than any other age groups.

Not only did drug manufacturers hide documents recording these dangers, they also altered documents they made available to the public. In May 2000, the *Boston Globe* reported that researchers at Eli Lilly, Prozac's manufacturer, changed documents to make Prozac's side effects seem less severe. In official documentation submitted to the FDA when the company first sought Prozac's approval, the company's record of a trial patient's suicide attempt was changed to "overdose" and the phrase "suicidal thoughts" was changed to depression. Eli Lilly supervisors felt the small number of adverse instances recorded wasn't statistically significant enough to warrant concern. Government regulators felt differently.

Once these issues came to light, officials quickly intervened. After reviewing these previously unreleased records documenting adverse reactions, British authorities banned doctors in England from prescribing SSRIs for children and teens. Canadian and American officials required drug makers to issue warnings on all SSRI drug product labels. In Canada, all SSRIs' labels had to contain a specific warning stating that the drugs could cause "severe agitation-type adverse events coupled with self-harm and harm to others" in some adults and children. In the United States, the FDA issued similar

> **Fast Fact**
>
> *One out of every hundred patients (previously non-suicidal patients) who took Prozac in clinical trials developed severe anxiety and agitation, causing them to attempt or commit suicide during the studies.*
>
> (Source: Eli Lilly documentation provided to the Boston Globe)

*Is Prozac good—or evil?*

labeling requirements and developed publications to educate consumers about the risks.

Though the FDA's *Medication Guide: About Using Antidepressants in Children and Teenagers* clearly states the risks of taking antidepressants, it discusses the benefits of drug treatment as well. It takes a cautious, balanced approach. It also reminds readers that of all current antidepressants available in the United States today, only fluoxetine (Prozac) has been approved by the FDA to treat depression in children and teens.

Now that Prozac and other SSRIs have been on the market for nearly two decades, we know more about what they do to the human body over longer periods of time. For some, SSRIs remain a miracle cure: giving patients lives beyond depression with minimal side effects. For others, SSRIs seem more like a cruel **paradox**: they alleviate depression or anxiety disorders, but they add a new set of problems for which the patients never asked.

So which is it? Are SSRIs a miracle cure, paradox, or violence-inducing evil? How can the consumer know? The situation becomes even more confusing when media and advertising enter the picture.

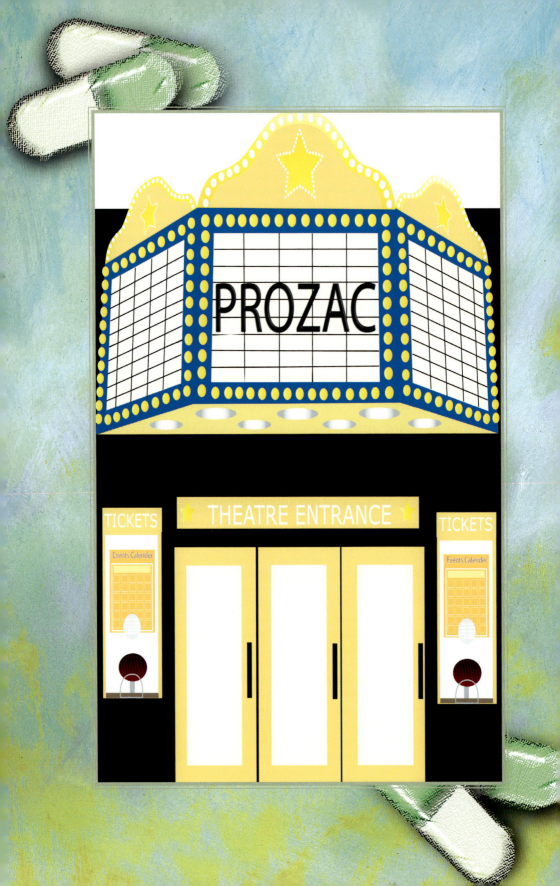

# Chapter 5

# *Prozac, Commercials, and Consumers: How Drug Marketing Impacts Culture*

*D*epression hurts . . . but you don't have to. Imagine a life that feels more manageable. Enjoying today and looking forward to tomorrow.
*If you have depression, this might seem out of reach. There is hope. . . .*

*#1 For Millions of Reasons*
*Zoloft® is safe and effective for the treatment of depression and anxiety. Why? It's the #1 doctor-prescribed brand of its kind. Zoloft has treated millions of people with more types of depression and anxiety than any brand of its kind for over 12 years. And Zoloft is available in multiple strengths, so your doctor can decide the right dose for you.*

*Find out if Zoloft could help you.*
*Ask your doctor about Zoloft today.*

Since the introduction of Prozac® in 1986, Lilly has helped over 50 million patients worldwide, and has earned a reputation for industry leadership in the treatment of depression and other neurological conditions.

Today Lilly continues to develop depression medications including treatments for:

- Both the emotional and painful physical symptoms of depression
- Difficult to treat depressive symptoms
- Symptoms of **bipolar disorder**

Only your doctor can determine which medication is right for you.

In the complex world of depression, look to Lilly for answers that matter.

*I'm ready to experience life.*
*WELLBUTRIN XL® works for my depression with a low risk of weight gain and sexual side effects.*
*Your results may vary.*

Do these advertisements sound familiar? If so, chances are you've seen them on television, heard them on the radio, or read them in magazines, newspapers, or on the Internet. Each promotes an antidepressant drug using what the FDA calls "direct-to-consumer" (DTC) advertising, a sales strategy designed to make consumers aware of the medications advertised so they'll ask their doctors to prescribe them.

Antidepressant manufacturers like those who make Prozac aren't the only companies to market their products directly to people who might use them; most prescription and over-the-counter (OTC) drug manufacturers do, too. Do you recognize these slogans?

*Are migraines disrupting your life?* (Imitrex®, a prescription medication to relieve migraine headaches)

*Keep that spark alive.* (Viagra®, a prescription medication to help correct erectile dysfunction)

*Live Claritin® clear.* (a once-prescription-now-OTC allergy relief medication)

*Quitting smoking is tough. But it doesn't have to be brutal.* (NicoDerm® CQ® nicotine patch)

*The healing purple pill.* (for Nexium®, a prescription drug for acid reflux disease)

*Virtually pain free.* (FreeStyle Flash® Blood Glucose Meters)

These represent only a few of the current advertising slogans for drug products marketed directly to consumers. Fifteen years ago you wouldn't have seen or heard a single commercial like these. For decades, prescription drug manufacturers advertised only to doctors who wrote prescriptions. Since doctors alone made drug treatment decisions, it made sense to direct sales pitches to them.

In the early 1980s, however, companies started directing their prescription drug advertisements toward ordinary people. In 1981, the first product-specific prescription drug ad ran in newspapers and magazines (for a pain-relief anti-inflammatory called Rufen®). During the next two years, television ads for that and other prescription drugs followed.

*In the nineteenth century, medicine was not regulated by the government.*

Consumers responded to these advertisements with so much interest that the FDA felt it needed to develop additional guidelines for DTC advertising. The FDA wanted to ensure the accuracy of the drug information provided in DTC ads and guard the safety of potential consumers. The regulating agency's concern was so great that between 1983 and 1985 the FDA requested all drug manufacturers to voluntarily stop DTC advertising for prescription drugs all together. The FDA did not want to return to the days of unregulated or misleading drug advertising.

## Advertising Rules: Why We Need Them and Where They Came From

Before the FDA came into being, marketing was an "anything goes" business. In the early 1900s, drug manufacturers could claim whatever they wanted about their products, whether it was true or not. Selling what they called "patent" medicines (drugs made with England's king's permission and funds, called patents, and imported to the United States), these manufacturers sold everything from miracle cures to exotic life enhancements.

Imagine reading this early 1900s advertisement:

*ECKMAN'S ALTERNATIVE for all throat and lung diseases including bronchitis, bronchial catarrh [inflammation], asthma, hay fever, coughs and colds, and catarrhs of the stomach and bowels, and tuberculosis (consumption).*

Would you believe this ad's claim that one to two teaspoons three to four times per day of this two-dollar-per-bottle serum could cure everything from lung disease to diarrhea? Of course not! But that's due largely to modern educational standards and consumer protections found in today's advertising laws. People in the late nineteenth and early twentieth century had no such protections.

Two pieces of legislation gave the public the safeguards it needed from unscrupulous drug makers and advertisers: the 1906 Pure Food and Drug Act, which required product labels to list all ingredients and ingredient strengths accurately (they couldn't include something in the product that they didn't list on the label), and the Food Drug and Cosmetic Act of 1938, which required companies to prove a drug was safe before they could market it to the public. Another 1938 legislation, the Wheeler-Lea Act, gave the U.S. Federal Trade Commission (FTC) jurisdiction over all drug advertising. This meant drug makers had to make sure their drugs' labels and advertisements provided information about their drugs according to FTC guidelines or they could face legal prosecution. In 1951, another piece of legislation, the Durham-Humphrey Amendment, established two broad categories of drugs: those safe enough to be sold directly to the consumer (what we now call over-the-counter drugs or OTCs) and those requiring a doctor's direct supervision (what we now call prescription drugs because they can only be sold by the request of and under the care of a licensed physician). In 1962, the FTC gave control of prescription drug labeling and advertising to the FDA.

While today's FDA advertising laws are quite detailed, we can sum up current guidelines this way: drug ads, whether for prescription or OTC drugs, must be accurate, truthful, complete, supported by science, and not misleading. In 1997, the FDA revised guidelines for DTC advertisements even further,

## Skyrocketing Advertising

*The Henry J. Kaiser Family Foundation, a private, nonprofit foundation focusing on major health-care issues facing Americans today, provided this assessment of DTC advertising in a 2001 report called Prescription Drug Trends by Larry Levitt:*

- *Between 1994 and 2000, spending by pharmaceutical companies for print and television DTC advertising increased from $266 million to $2.5 billion, a nearly ten-fold increase in less than seven years.*

- *In 2000 pharmaceutical companies spent a total of $15.7 billion on marketing and promotions, a number representing 14 percent of their total drug sales. Other industries spent far less: department stores spent only 3.7 percent of their total sales on advertising; tobacco products, only 3.9 percent.*

- *From 1993 to 2000 public awareness of DTC drug advertisements increased from 39 percent to over 90 percent. This means that in 1993 only four out of every ten people said they had heard or seen an ad for a prescription medication. By the year 2000, nine out of ten recalled having seen or heard these ads.*

*Three-quarters of all doctors surveyed said that their patients speak to them about advertisements they've seen or heard.*

requiring that drug advertisements include not only a drug's benefits and indicated usages, but also its risks and potential adverse or unwanted side effects. The guidelines require "fair balance": that is, FDA reviewers examine advertisements to make sure they provide a balanced description of both a drug's risks and benefits. Risks cannot be overlooked or minimized; benefits cannot be exaggerated. The 1997 revisions and the relaxed permissions these revisions provided for advertising prescription drugs directly to consumers resulted in dramatic increases in the amount of DTC advertising since then.

This increase in DTC advertising is why the advertising phrases and slogans opening this chapter seem familiar. In one 1996 study, cited in the 1998 FDA report *Direct to You: TV Drug Ads that Make Sense* by Tamar Nordenberg, three-quarters of the doctors surveyed said their patients had spoken to them about drugs they'd heard or seen advertised. In other words, people saw ads for specific drug products and then initiated discussions with their doctors about them. Drug manufacturers realized if they advertised prescription drugs to the ordinary people who needed them, these people would ask their doctors for the drugs they'd seen advertised, doctors would write more prescriptions for the requested drugs, and the drug manufacturers would make more money. *The greater the public awareness*, this drug company thinking goes, *the greater the profits will be*. Advertisements also provided consumers with education on the illnesses themselves, showing them how to recognize the symptoms and instructing them to then talk to their doctors and ask for a particular medicine.

Market studies indicate that pharmaceutical companies spend more money today on DTC advertising than at any time in history. The goal is make individuals aware of drugs once marketed only to the doctors who prescribe them.

This practice of marketing prescription drugs directly to consumers, according to the FDA, results in consequences both good and bad.

## The Good and Bad of Advertising

People who need prescription drugs benefit from knowing more about them. Informed patients generally make better decisions about health care. Some researchers and consumer advocates see advertisements as allowing ordinary people to take more responsibility for their health issues and drug treatments. Knowing a drug exists, they suggest, encourages a patient to discuss his condition more with his doctor, not less. The patient knows more about his options and feels more confident discussing them.

Other researchers see widespread DTC prescription-drug advertising as potentially dangerous, suggesting that ad-informed patients may pressure doctors to prescribe unnecessary or inappropriate drugs they've seen on TV or that they may expect advertised drugs to provide easy fixes for complicated medical issues as their advertisements often portray them.

To investigate the debate, FDA researchers surveyed physicians and patients about DTC advertising between 1999 and 2002. In the *Summary of FDA Survey Research Results* issued in November 2004, the FDA concluded that DTC advertising could affect doctor–patient relationships in positive and negative ways. Positive aspects the FDA identified included these: DTC ads gave patients greater awareness of diseases and treatments; they motivated patients to learn more about their conditions; and they equipped patients to ask better questions of their health-care providers. The drawbacks, on the other hand, troubled FDA researchers: half of the physicians surveyed felt their patients pressured them to prescribe

*Better-informed patients can discuss their options more intelligently with their doctors.*

## American Medical Association's Guidelines for DTC Advertising

*During an FDA public hearing held in 2005, pharmacologist Joseph Cranston provided this summary of the American Medical Association's (AMA) guidelines for acceptable DTC advertising:*

*"In brief, the AMA currently believes that a DTC ad is acceptable if it is disease specific, it enhances patient education, it presents a scientifically accurate message, and exhibits fair balance between benefit and risk information, is understandable by consumers, promotes discussion between patient and physician rather than encouraging self diagnosis and self treatment, and is run only after physicians have been appropriately educated about the drug. . . . However, the AMA is preparing a new report on DTC and its policy will be revisited in June, 2006."*

DTC-advertised drugs; patients and doctors alike felt most ads exaggerated the drugs' effectiveness and presented unbalanced views of the drugs' risks and benefits; nearly two-thirds of the doctors felt DTC ads led patients to question their doctors' diagnoses, and more than one-fourth said DTC advertising caused problems for their patients and their medical practices.

Prozac was and is no exception in the debate about DTC advertising's influence. Introduced to the American public after FDA approval in 1987, Prozac advertising changed the way Americans think about mental illness. Commercials for Prozac described depressive disorders as treatable biological conditions. Media advertisements and front-page coverage on the 1990 issues of *Newsweek* and *New Yorker* magazines touted the new antidepressant as a "wonder drug," a medical "breakthrough," and a "miracle cure" for depression. Some called the little capsules "happy pills" because previously depressed patients said Prozac made them feel "better than well." Prozac, much media coverage claimed, could help not only depression, but personality issues *not* rooted in mental illness: shyness, social awkwardness, timidity, and introverted tendencies. People began to believe Prozac could turn shy wallflowers into popular social butterflies. The new

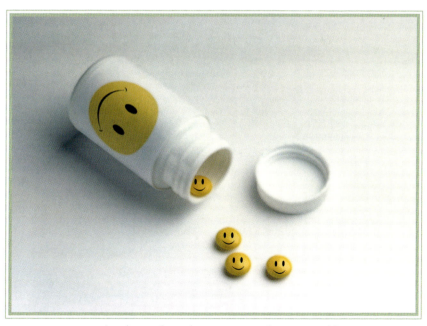

*People thought of Prozac as "happy pills."*

antidepressant could not only treat people with depression, the media suggested, it could improve the personalities of the nondepressed.

As media coverage spread the word of Prozac's purported wonder-working capabilities, demand for it grew. Prozac became the drug of choice for celebrities. Taking the new antidepressant became a socially popular and acceptable thing to do; a status no previous mental health medication ever enjoyed. Within two years, by 1989, pharmacies were filling 65,000 Prozac prescriptions *per month*. Within five years, 4.5

*More than 54 million prescriptions have been filled for Prozac!*

million Americans had tried the drug. Today, nearly two decades later, Eli Lilly estimates that doctors have prescribed Prozac for 54 million people worldwide.

Prozac's widespread advertising and media coverage made the new antidepressant and clinical depression household terms. Psychiatric medications, once prescribed primarily by psychiatrists and reserved only for the most severely mentally ill, became routine treatment **protocols** for the mildly depressed, prescribed as often by family doctors as by physicians specializing in mental health disorders.

"Because of Prozac's widespread publicity," comments psychiatrist Karl Benzio, "patients weren't as reluctant to try antidepressants as they had been before." He continues:

> They'd heard of more and more people taking Prozac with phenomenal results and few side effects, so this new class of depression medications seemed safe to try. Many people were willing to seek and accept help for depression, even milder forms, than would have been were it not for the popularity of this new class of drugs.
>
> Prozac had its downsides, too. People saw it as a quick fix. After taking the drug, if patients experienced symptom reduction in depression or anxiety disorders, they assumed drug treatment was the only treatment they needed, when in fact they were overlooking other contributing factors.

Dr. Benzio's comment reveals the problem with most media advertisements. Because they're designed to fill a ten-second or thirty-second slot and to appeal to the masses, commercials can't go into detail. Most media consultants strive for a sound bite or pithy saying to capture their products, especially since they know they have mere seconds to grab the consumer's attention. The same holds true for the average mass-media article. The current keep-it-light, -short, and -easy-to-read mentality behind most periodical publications doesn't allow for much detail. The average reader, because of depression's light media treatment, sees depression as an easily treated brain-chemical problem that can be corrected by popping a daily (or weekly) pill.

Nothing could be further from the truth.

"People are not just beings of chemistry," Dr. Benzio explains.

> We have spirits and minds and bodies. And while medications affect the biochemistry of psychiatric disorders, they don't address root issues or underlying causes: behavioral issues, thought processes, false beliefs, other health issues and psychodynamic elements. So when patients see drugs like Prozac as panaceas, they skip other necessary treatment avenues, such as behavioral therapy or cognitive therapy, because of the false security the drugs provide. The patients who rely solely on drug therapy without other interventions rarely experience complete recovery.

That's a truth popular media rarely covers.

## Reclaiming Truth and Accuracy

While the FDA controls truth and accuracy in drug advertising, it does not regulate article content in magazines, newspapers, or news stories aired on television and radio. Here is where the consumer needs to be most discerning. It may seem like a lot of work, but to get at the truth behind a drug's media hype the consumer needs to do her research. She can check sources cited in articles. She can find and read the original sources of content quoted in articles. She can read literature

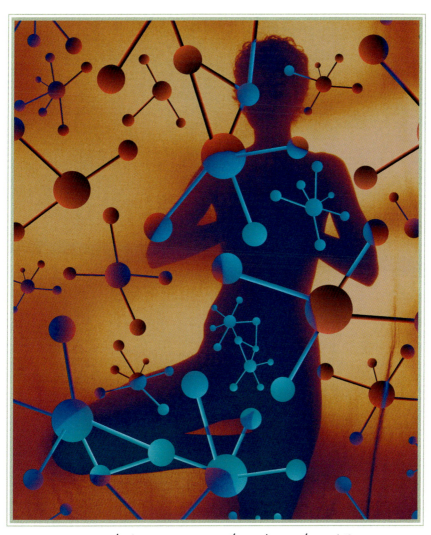

*Human beings are more than just chemistry.*

*Your doctor is employed by you.*

from reputable, more objective organizations concerned with public welfare: U.S. National Institutes of Health (NIH), U.S. National Institute of Mental Health (NIMH), U.S. Centers for Disease Control and Prevention (CDC), U.S. Food and Drug Administration (FDA), U.S. National Library of Medicine (NLM), Health Canada; Health Canada's MedEffect initiative, the American Psychological Association (APA), and the Mayo Clinic are just a few. And she should *always* discuss medications with her doctor or health-care provider. Remember, a doctor is in *the patient's* employ; patients pay him for his services. Part of what a patient pays him for is instruction and information about medications the patient may need. Patients can ask questions and can keep asking until they receive the answers they need.

Yes, media coverage provides much information about drugs and their intended uses, and consumers can benefit from the information they obtain about prescription drugs from media sources. The information provided in popular media, however, is necessarily incomplete and can sometimes be inaccurate. Consumers need to check other sources and talk to their doctors. The more accurate the information a patient gathers about a potential drug treatment, the more equipped the patient will be to assess the drugs' risks and benefits and whether or not the drug is the right drug for her.

## Chapter 6

# Beyond Prozac: What's Next for Psychiatric Medications?

*I*n 10,000 BCE, tribal healers treated those with psychiatric illnesses by drilling holes in their heads to release the spirits troubling their minds.

Ancient Egyptians used herbs, spices, and religious avenues of prayer and sacrifice to help the mentally ill.

Early Roman physicians treated mental illness with soothing music and isolation.

Second-century Greeks treated manic-depression with mineral water baths.

During the Middle Ages, psychiatric patients had their mental illnesses beaten or tortured out of them.

In the 1700s and early 1800s, psychiatric patients ended up in sanitariums, warehouses for the insane, but they at least received more humane care there than they'd received at any other time before in history.

By the late 1800s, doctors had discovered the sedating effects of certain drugs and often used morphine to sedate psychiatric patients.

In the 1900s, doctors tried electroshock therapy (ECT), in which electrical currents were sent through the patient's brain to treat psychiatric disorders.

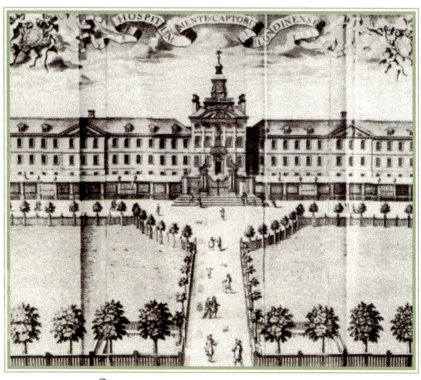

*In London, in the 1700s, people with mental disorders were locked away within Bedlam, an enormous warehouse for the insane.*

Finally, in the mid-twentieth century, researchers discovered the first truly psychiatric drugs.

It's taken literally millennia of human history to pave the way for drug-treatment breakthroughs in psychiatric medications. But once the doors opened in the mid-1950s, advances in psychiatric medicines came swiftly.

In the twenty-first century, depression treatments and psychiatric drug classes continue to evolve. We've seen how health-care providers for people with depression initially depended on two early classes of antidepressants: the MAOIs and tricyclics discovered only a half-century ago. Then Prozac, introduced in the 1980s, came along as one of the first of a new class of drugs: the SSRIs. Prozac and the other SSRIs opened new fields of study in brain chemistry and how certain drugs impact neurotransmitters. What researchers discovered, however, was that they hadn't yet identified all the neurotransmitters in the brain.

> **Fast Fact**
>
> Because most psychiatric disorders involve more than one of the brain's neurotransmitters, more than 50 percent of psychiatric patients take more than one psychiatric drug to manage their symptoms.

As doctors discovered the existence of these additional neurotransmitters and learned about their roles in brain chemistry, further classes of antidepressants ensued: the SNRIs

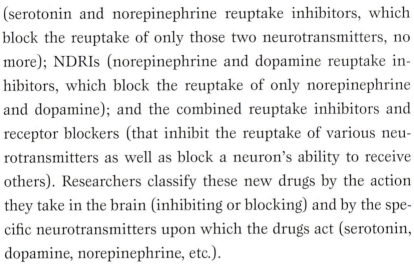

(serotonin and norepinephrine reuptake inhibitors, which block the reuptake of only those two neurotransmitters, no more); NDRIs (norepinephrine and dopamine reuptake inhibitors, which block the reuptake of only norepinephrine and dopamine); and the combined reuptake inhibitors and receptor blockers (that inhibit the reuptake of various neurotransmitters as well as block a neuron's ability to receive others). Researchers classify these new drugs by the action they take in the brain (inhibiting or blocking) and by the specific neurotransmitters upon which the drugs act (serotonin, dopamine, norepinephrine, etc.).

And the search for newer, better antidepressants continues. Some newer drugs have become available in other countries but are not yet available in Canada and the United States where they are still under review by governing agencies. These drugs may prove to be the next wonder drugs for depressive illnesses, but only time will tell. In the meantime, pharmaceutical companies all over the world invest billions of dollars in clinical research and the development of new drugs: ones they hope will work better and cause fewer side effects.

Until the next breakthrough in psychiatric medications occurs, patients have to rely on the many effective drugs already approved for treating their mental disorders. Although these drugs may have side effects, education can help people be aware of dangerous symptoms. With the amount of media coverage and advertising available today, patients can also make informed decisions about the drugs they and their

*Developing new medications costs millions of dollars.*

doctors choose. If the first drugs tried don't work, they can try others. If one class of antidepressants causes too many side effects, patients have alternate classes to which they can look for symptom relief.

Doctors agree that many patients respond best not to a single medication but to a combination of therapies regardless of the medications they choose. Research supports their conclusion. In his work *Better Than Prozac: Creating the Next Generation of Psychiatric Drugs* Samuel H. Barondes cites a 1997 study done by the American Psychiatric Association that illustrates just how common the practice of combining psychiatric drugs is when treating patients with psychiatric illnesses. The replies of the 417 psychiatrists surveyed indicated that more than 50 percent of their patients used more than one psychiatric drug at a time; almost a third used a combination of three or more to treat their symptoms. Current treatment philosophy believes that drugs used in conjunction with one another, rather than single medications used alone, may offer greater benefits to some patients. And not only should drugs be used in combination with other drugs, but drug treatment should also be used in combination with other therapies (such as talk therapy and exercise).

As Dr. Barondes concludes:

> the results [for the depressed person] will not come all at once. It may take many years to accumulate and integrate the relevant material [from various studies]. It may take many more years to translate these discoveries into new psychiatric remedies.

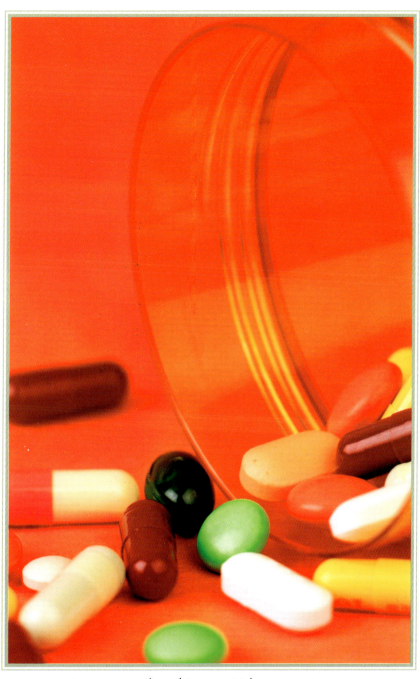

*Many people taking antidepressants use more than one kind of medication.*

## Current MAOIs
## (Monamine Oxidase Inhibitors)

| Generic Name | Brand Name |
| --- | --- |
| isocarboxazid | Marplan |
| phenelzine | Nardil |
| tranylcypromine | Parnate |

## Current SSRIs
## (Selective Serotonin Reuptake Inhibitors)

| Generic Name | Brand Name |
| --- | --- |
| citalopram | Celexa |
| escitalopram | Lexapro |
| fluoxetine | Prozac |
| fluvoxamine | Luvox |
| faroxetine | Paxil |
| sertraline | Zoloft |

## Current SNRIs
## (Serotonin and Norepinephrine Reuptake Inhibitors)

| Generic Name | Brand Name |
| --- | --- |
| duloxetine | Cymbalta |
| venlafaxine | Effexor and Effexor XR |

## Current NDRIs
## (Norepinephrine and Dopamine Reuptake Inhibitors)

**Generic Name**  
bupropion

**Brand Name**  
Wellbutrin  
Wellbutrin XL and Wellbutrin SR  
Zyban

## Current Combined Action Antidepressants
## (Combined Reuptake Inhibitors and Receptor Blockers)

**Generic Name**  
trazodone  
nefazodone  
mirtazpine  
maprotiline

**Brand Name**  
Desyrel  
Serzone  
Remeron  
Ludiomil

# Prozac: North American Culture and the Wonder Drug

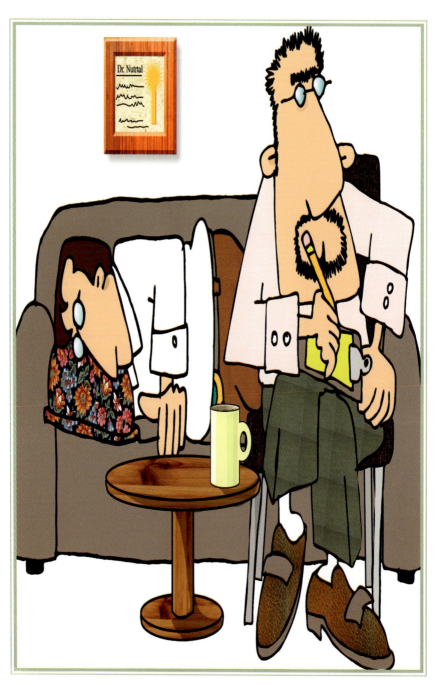

*Today, people with mental disorders have many more options available to them.*

In the meantime, thanks in part to Prozac's influence on psychiatry, as well as the general public's perception of the mind and mental health, people with psychiatric illnesses today have safer and far more treatment options (drugs and other therapies combined) from which to choose than their predecessors ever had. And they're seeing far greater results.

# Further Reading

Appleton, William S. *Prozac and the New Antidepressants: What You Need to Know About Prozac, Zoloft, Paxil, Luvox, Wellbutrin, Effexor, Serzone, Vestra, Celexa, St. John's Wort, and Others (Revised Edition)*. New York: Plume, 2000.

Drummond, Edward. *The Complete Guide to Psychiatric Drugs: Straight Talk for Best Results*. New York: John Wiley and Sons, Inc., 2000.

Esherick, Joan. *Drug Therapy and Mood Disorders*. Broomall, Pa.: Mason Crest, 2004.

Esherick, Joan. *The FDA and Psychiatric Drugs: How a Drug Is Approved*. Broomall, Pa.: Mason Crest, 2004.

Glenmullen, Joseph. *Prozac Backlash: Overcoming the Dangers of Prozac, Zoloft, Paxil, and Other Antidepressants with Safe, Effective Alternatives*. New York: Simon and Schuster, 2000.

Griffith, H. Winter, and Stephen Moore, eds. *Complete Guide to Prescription and Nonprescription Drugs, 2006 Edition*. New York: Perigee, 2005.

Margolis, Simeon, ed. *The Johns Hopkins Complete Home Guide to Pills and Medicines*. New York: Black Dog and Leventhal, 2005.

Morrison, James. *DSM-IV Made Easy: The Clinician's Guide to Diagnosis*. New York: Guildford, 2001.

# For More Information

American Psychiatric Association
www.psych.org

American Psychological Association
www.apa.org

Eli Lilly and Company
www.prozac.com

Health Canada
www.hc-sc.gc.ca

National Alliance for the Mentally Ill
www.nami.org

National Depressive and Manic-Depressive Association
www.ndmda.org

National Institute of Mental Health
www.nimh.nih.gov

National Institutes of Health
www.nih.gov

National Library of Medicine
www.nlm.nih.gov

National Library of Medicine's Fluoxetine Information Page
www.nlm.nih.gov/medlineplus/druginfo/medmaster/a689006.html

*For More Information*

National Mental Health Association
www.nmha.org

National Mental Health Information Center
www.mentalhealth.org

United States Food and Drug Administration
www.fda.gov

United States Surgeon General's Report on Mental Health
www.surgeongeneral.gov/library/mentalhealth

# Glossary

***axon:*** A thread-like extension of a neuron.

***behavioral therapy:*** A psychological treatment method that focuses on behavior.

***bipolar disorder:*** A psychological disorder characterized by periods of extreme emotional highs and lows.

***clinical trials:*** In the drug-approval process, the period in which the drug is tested in humans.

***cognitive therapy:*** A psychological treatment method that focuses on thought processes.

***dissipate:*** To fade or disappear.

***manic:*** Having to do with a state of abnormally high excitement and energy, rapid thinking and speech, and exaggerated ideas of self.

***nuances:*** Very slight differences in meaning, feeling, tone, or color.

***paradox:*** A statement or situation that seems to be absurd or contradictory but is or may be true.

***postoperative shock:*** A state where the vital processes associated with blood volume and blood pressure are extremely diminished that appears after surgery.

***protocols:*** Detailed plans of a scientific or medical experiment, treatment, or procedure.

***psychodynamics:*** The interactions of the emotional and motivational forces that affect behavior and mental states, especially subconsciously.

***psychotherapy:*** The use of talking and analysis to treat mental disorders.

***schizophrenia:*** A psychological disorder characterized by a loss of contact with reality.

# Bibliography

Appleton, William S. *The New Antidepressants and Antianxieties*. New York: Penguin Group, 2004.

Breggin, Peter R. *The Antidepressant Fact Book: What Your Doctor Won't Tell You About Prozac, Zoloft, Paxil, Celexa, and Luvox*. Cambridge, Mass.: Perseus Publishing, 2001.

Carey, Benedict. "Is Prozac a Safer Antidepressant?" *International Herald Tribune*, September 23, 2004.

Carey, Benedict. "Prozac or Talk for Troubled Teens." *International Herald Tribune*, June 10, 2004.

Crowley, Mary. "Do Kids Need Prozac?" *Newsweek*, October 20, 1997.

Elias, Marilyn. "Prozac Linked to Child Suicide Risk." *USA Today*, September 15, 2004.

Elliott, Carl, and Tod Chambers (eds.). *Prozac as a Way of Life*. Chapel Hill: University of North Carolina Press, 2004.

Feldman, Martin. "SSRIs: Are They Safe as Promised?" *Townsend Letter for Doctors and Patients*, May 1, 2004.

Helms, Marisa. "Shooting Fuels Debate Over Safety of Prozac." http://news.minnesota.publicradio.org/features/2005/03/25_helmsm_prozacfolo.

Kramer, Peter D. *Listening to Prozac: The Landmark Book About Anti-Depressants and the Remaking of the Self*. New York: Penguin Group, 1997.

Mundell, E. J. "Prozac Appears Safe, Effective in Teens." *Health Day*, June 2, 2004.

"Prozac in Children." *Pediatrics for Parents*, July 1, 1997.

Williams, Jason. "Prozac Before Puberty." *Psychology Today*, March 1, 2003.

Wurtzel, Elizabeth. *Prozac Nation: Young and Depressed in America*. New York: Penguin Group, 2002.

# Index

advertising rules 83–88
agitation 25
American Medical Association (AMA) 90
American Psychiatric Association 104
American Psychological Association (APA) 97
antihistamines 24, 25, 27, 28,
anxiety 15, 25, 55
axon 36

behavioral therapy 18, 20, 48, 51–52
brompheniramine 28
bulimia nervosa 14

Celexa (citalopram) 106
Claritin 81
clinical trials 74
cognitive therapy 18, 20, 48–51
cognitive-behavioral therapy 48, 52
combined reuptake inhibitors 107
Cymbalta (duloxetine) 106

dendrites 37
Desyrel (trazodone) 107
direct to consumer advertising (DTC) 80–81, 83, 85, 87, 88, 89, 90
dopamine 27, 72, 102
drug approval 12
drug warnings 29, 75, 77
Durham-Humphrey Amendment 84
dyskinesia 70

Effexor and Effexor XR (venlafaxine) 106

Eldepryl 14
electroshock therapy (ECT) 100
Eli Lilly pharmaceutical company 22, 28, 29, 75, 80, 93

facial tics 70, 72, 73–74
faith-based activities 59–61, 62
Food and Drug Administration (FDA) 12, 15, 22, 29, 74, 75, 77, 80, 83, 84, 85, 87, 88, 89, 91, 94, 97
Food, Drug and Cosmetic Act of 1983 84

Health Canada 97
*House* 42, 44

Imitrex 81
iproniazid 22, 25, 26

Lexapro (escitalopram) 106
life coaching 54–55
light therapy (phototherapy) 57
lithium 22
Ludiomil (maprotiline) 107
Luvox (fluvoxamine) 106

major depressive disorder 14
manic 25
Marplan (isocarboxazid) 14, 106
Mayo Clinic 97
Middle Ages, the 99
monoamine oxidase inhibitors (MAOIs) 14, 26, 101, 106

Nardil (phenelzine) 14, 106
natural remedies 61–62
neurons 14, 33, 37
neurotransmitters 27, 28, 29, 36, 37, 38, 39, 72, 101, 102

Nexium 81
NicoDerm CQ 81
norepinephrine 28, 102
norepinephrine and dopamine reuptake inhibitors (NDRIs) 102, 107

obsessive-compulsive disorder (OCD) 14

Parnate (tranylcypromine) 14, 106
Paxil (faroxetine) 106
postsynaptic neuron 36, 37
premenstrual dysphoric disorder (PMDD) 14
presynaptic neurons 36, 37
psychiatric treatment 17–21
psychodynamic investigation 53–54
psychotherapy 23
Pure Food and Drug Act (1906) 84

receptor blockers 107
Remeron (mirtazpine) 107
reuptake 28, 38, 39, 102
Rufen 82

sanitariums 100
Sarafam 14
schizophrenia 23
seasonal affective disorder (SAD) 57–58
selective serotonin reuptake inhibitors (SSRIs) 14, 18, 28, 41, 44, 45, 47, 63, 68, 71, 74, 75, 77, 101, 106
serotonin 28, 39, 44, 56, 57, 58, 71, 102

serotonin and norepinephrine reuptake inhibitors (SNRIs) 102
serotonin syndrome 39–45
Serzone (nefazodone) 107
side effects of Prozac 9, 14, 15, 63, 65–77
suicide 68, 69, 74, 75
synapse 28, 36, 39

talk therapy 18, 20, 52–53
Therapeutic Product Directorate (TPD) 12
Thorazine (chlorpromazine) 25, 26
tricyclic antidepressants (TCAs) 26, 101
tuberculosis 22, 25

U.S. Centers for Disease Control and Prevention (CDC) 97
U.S. Federal Trade Commission (FTC) 84
U.S. National Institute of Mental Health (NIMH)
U.S. National Institutes of Health (NIH) 97
U.S. National Library of Medicine (NLM) 97

Viagra 81

Wellbutrin, Wellbutrin XL and Wellbutrin SR, and Zyban (bupropion) 80, 107
Wheeler-Lea Act 84
World Health Organization (WHO) 21, 23

Zelmid (zimelidine) 22, 28
Zoloft (sertraline) 79, 106
Zyban (bupropion) 80, 107

## Picture Credits

Benjamin Stewart: pp. 21, 27
iStockphotos: pp. 8, 11, 13, 15, 17, 19, 49, 55, 56, 58, 78, 98
    Arne Thaysen: p. 66
    Camilo Jimenez: p. 44
    Dale Taylor: p. 64
    Dennis Cox: p. 108
    Elvis Wilson: p. 86
    Frances Twitty: p. 103
    Irene Chan: p. 53
    Kenn Wislander: p. 73
    Luis Carlos Torres: p. 38
    Mark Stay: p. 69
    Miroslaw Pieprzyk: p. 71
    Sherry Schuller: p. 50
    Tambolbee Toting: p. 76
    Trudy Karl: p. 46
Jupiter Images: pp. 40, 43, 89, 91, 92, 95, 96, 105
Malinda Miller: pp. 33, 37
National Library of Medicine: pp. 24, 82

# Biographies

## Author

Joan Esherick works as the Chief Writer and Managing Editor for Lighthouse Network, a nonprofit organization specializing in mental health education and training. She is also the author of twenty-five nonfiction books including *Drug Therapy and Mood Disorders, The FDA and Psychiatric Drugs: How a Drug is Approved,* and several others about psychiatric drugs and mental health issues. Happily married for twenty-five years and the mother of three nearly grown children, Joan knows the importance of maintaining her mental health. She does so by combining her prescribed drug treatment with regular exercise, healthy eating habits, faith involvement, and enjoyment of her three Labrador retrievers. You can read about their adventures on Joan's blog Lab Tails, found at http://labtails.blogspot.com.

## Consultant

Andrew M. Kleiman, M.D., received a Bachelor of Arts degree in philosophy from the University of Michigan, and earned his medical degree from Tulane University School of Medicine. Dr. Kleiman completed his internship, residency in psychiatry, and fellowship in forensic psychiatry at New York University and Bellevue Hospital. He is currently in private practice in Manhattan, specializing in psychopharmacology, psychotherapy, and forensic psychiatry. He also teaches clinical psychology at the New York University School of Medicine.